One Bright Day in the Middle of the Night

Ptr J. D. Swanson

PAGE PUBLISHING
Conneaut Lake, PA

First originally published by Page Publishing 2024

ISBN 979-8-88793-782-3 (pbk)
ISBN 979-8-89157-726-8 (hc)
ISBN 979-8-88793-793-9 (digital)

Printed in the United States of America

Acknowledgments

Thanks to Life Christian University and Dr. Windgate, a brother in Christ. Your friendship and leadership have inspired me and many others. God bless.

Thank you, Pastor Chris Marshall, for your dedication and determination and for helping edit the manuscript.

Special thanks to the writers and authors of the Bible. Without their leadership and dedication, this would not all be possible.

Special thanks to Brother Bill and Harold Junior of Wofr.org radio station, who spread the news in over 175 countries, FM and AM, through various apps, and for prison ministries on radio FM network. All stations are on the World Wide Web. Please, if you can, donate to Wofr.org broadcasting. Thank you.

Contents

1

Light Will Prevail

On a cool, fall night, the stars shone brilliantly against the dark-blue sky. The previous New Year's Eve had made history. When you have faith, hope glimmers every moment.

Most of us are not aware that in biblical times, days started in the evening, and morning followed. The Genesis's account of creation illustrates this truth. After each day of God's creative work, we read: "There was evening and morning, the first day…There was evening and morning, the second day…There was evening and morning…"

In the middle of the night in a small mining town, everyone knew a familiar face. There was a familiar hope in the air as they were looking down on a small hospital bed in a nearby town, watching as the doctors and nurses tried to save this tiny baby's life. The baby's first day had started in the middle of the night. The medical staff worked to ensure it was not his last; God's hand was surely on this very small infant boy.

In the 1950s, a baby weighing one and a half pounds at birth held minute odds of surviving. When his mother first saw him, she said, "He's the size of a stick of butter."

For nearly six months, the baby lived in the little hospital bed. He awoke every day and watched the doctors and nurses perform their routines. Eventually, he came home to a family who lived in a small apartment above their family-run business.

My father's mechanic shop below meant the apartment experienced little quiet. The aroma of oil or fluids of some type filling the air, the noise of cars running, a large air compressor kicking on and off, or people talking could be heard from early morning until late at night. Only then did things get a little quieter.

When winter came, the air in the apartment stayed cool, to say the least. The furnace's thermostat, which hung on the wall down in the back bay of the garage, was always set very low. The same furnace heated the back rooms of their apartment.

The sound of little feet scampering quietly—so as not to wake up Dad, who worked twelve hours per day, seven days a week—interrupted the nighttime quiet. The furnace vent was located under Mom and Dad's bed to distribute any available heat where it was most needed and meant we crawled under the bed to keep warm at night.

From my earliest recollection, that cycle in the winter months changed very little. I was the small baby, and my little feet were the ones often heard scampering quietly so I could snuggle under the bed to soak up the heat.

The small town where we lived hid nestled in the mountains. Coal had been mined there from the eighteen hundreds into the early nineteen hundreds. The businesses in town included a small grocery store, a general store, a few pubs, and two gas stations.

Traveling to neighboring towns did not increase our choices in prices or apparel, so we shopped at the small grocery or general store. Buying clothes meant choosing from a catalogue at the general store. The clothes in the catalogue came with high prices and poor quality, not a particularly enticing combination.

Every year before school started, we ordered two pairs of pants and two shirts. They had to last the entire school year. I learned when I was older that my dad made monthly payments to afford those clothes. Despite such conditions, we never felt poor or deprived of anything as we grew up. The greatest joy in those years for us as children was being free and spending most of our time outside on some type of adventure.

As the years went by, I became friends with a neighbor who was my age. Matt lived up the road a short distance, just a couple hundred feet or so on the other side of the road at the bottom of a big hill. We were seven or eight years old when we became friends. Matt came from a large, poor family, much poorer than we were. Food was scarce for them. They had a big old bathtub hidden behind a cloth sheet in a back room. Sheets hung in the doorways of the house instead of doors. One of the mysteries the house held for me was the tub, which contained layers of peanut butter at the bottom. It was covered with a sheet of wood.

Matt's family got government-issued large cardboard containers filled with peanut butter. When we played at Matt's house and got hungry, his mom let us get crackers from a large can and scoop out the peanut butter.

One of our favorite activities in those days was taking our small toy cars and pushing them into a long black tube, which was six or eight inches in diameter and maybe twenty or so feet long. It rested on a steep hill behind Matt's house. We would see whose car rolled the farthest down the hill after it came out of the tube. We played this game thousands of times every summer.

Life rolled along that way without many cares. But one day, as I got ready to go outside and play, my mom told me I could not go. I didn't remember hearing the sirens or other loud noises that morning, but Mom told me my friend, Matt, was "gone." He had been crossing the road when a car hit him. Just like that, he was "gone." Matt's family observed no funeral. No one ever said a thing about the accident. The church we attended on Sundays was a mile or two away. The pastor was very old and perpetually grumpy. He never mentioned the accident either. I remember thinking, *Where did he go? I'll see him again someday.* I was not sure where, but someone reassured me I would see him again. That someone's assurance had been an anchor throughout my life.

As the years went by, I attended the school of hard knocks. I often found it hard to pass because the tests came before I learned the lessons. For example, sometimes battles come into our lives, and we do not see them coming. One such battle brewed for quite some time. It was not just a mental battle but a spiritual one as well. While neither type of battle shows visibly to the human eye, I could "see" the hostility and bitterness growing between my mother and grandpa. He lived across the street from us. While that seemed innocent enough, it proved to be the beginning of an extremely bad situation. She was like a volcano ready to erupt. The first time I witnessed the eruption, I was surprised. Something was not right, and although neither had ever shown any signs of aggressive hostility before—at least, I was not aware of any—it erupted.

As I grew older, I was recruited to help whenever any kind of work came up, which was quite often. I did not mind because except for playing baseball, not much activity took place where we lived.

The service station where my dad worked and which I thought he owned had a small office, which sold different items to the public. Candy bars and cigars sat in a long glass and wooden showcase. The candies included $100,000 Bars, Mallo Cups, Reese's Cups, and waxed tubes filled with different colors of flavored syrup. The cigars were the small Swisher sweet cigars, which my dad and uncle smoked or mostly chewed the ends all day.

The office also contained a small cooler with Fudgsicles, ice creams, sandwiches, and small cups of vanilla ice cream with fudge-like syrup on top. (Boy, were they good!) A cigarette machine, pop machine, and several nickel machines also stood in the office. I was not allowed to take any items without first receiving permission. Pop, my grandpa, was quite strict about that.

One of the bottles of pop they sold was called Moxie. It tasted different, with a kind of bitter birch-like flavor. My uncle liked it and said it tasted like real beer. We also sold snuff for a while, and some very strange-looking characters came in to buy the tobacco products. The first time I snuck some snuff with a couple friends, Pops said I turned every shade of green before I barfed.

The worst group of dudes who came in—I meant the worst—were some kind of "warriors," who belonged to a motorcycle gang. They committed more crimes by accident than most criminals committed in a lifetime. These guys had not shaved for a decade. They did not wear shirts, just vests with patches everywhere and tattoos everywhere with the name of their gang on the back. The name was centered on a big black cross.

They were a tough bunch, and no one messed with them. The big old Harleys they rode always needed work. My dad often fixed their bikes, and they said he really knew his stuff. My dad told them about how he rode motorcycles in the military. Dad seemed to get along with just about everyone.

Two gas pumps stood in front of the station. Gas sold for twenty-nine cents a gallon, and it stayed that price for years. Neither storms nor catastrophes changed the price. Imagine that. Things were so different back then. Politics had not yet destroyed our economy and our way of life.

We did not have television or FM radio. The radio only picked up one AM station. I had a little transistor radio I kept in my pocket. It measured about two by two inches and had a wire that led to a single earpiece. I bought it from an advertisement on the back cover of a comic book. It cost a quarter. I always tried to tune something in while I worked, but I usually only got static during the day.

The work included tending to the people who came to the service station. My dad told me to fill the cars with the amount of gas the customers wanted. That was a greater challenge than it might seemed because every car was different. In addition to having fill caps on the sides, some cars had them behind the license plates and some even had the fill caps behind the taillights. That made them nearly impossible to find. The guys hanging out would watch to see if I would find the fill cap right away or have to ask the driver where the cap was. That was the entertainment for the day.

A couple of retired guys usually hung around telling stories and being nebby. Everyone knew just about everyone else, and these guys had opinions on just how wrong everyone else was. If you do not believe them, just ask them. I found their stories about World War I and World War II to be extremely interesting.

They lived through far tougher times than I experienced, but they always talked of their families getting through the tough times together. In most of their conversations, church or ethnic groups came up in good ways.

Most of the churches in our area were Roman Catholic, and they had huge buildings compared to the Protestant churches. About two miles from our house was a convent where the nuns lived and a Catholic school. The church we attended was in the opposite direction. It was small with maybe thirty or forty people attending on a good Sunday.

My parents enrolled me in the confirmation class, which lasted two or three years. I did not remember exactly how long it lasted. All I knew was I thought it seemed way too long. Because our church was so small, we had to ride to a neighboring town to combine our confirmation class with another church's. They educated us in religion, but no one ever talked about healing or other spiritual beliefs. They told us God watched over us, and He was angry with us.

The men in our town seemed stern. They exhibited hard-core, stern demeanors. You seldom saw a smile from many of the older guys. The dress codes were simple: Guys wore white socks, dark pants, and they always wore shirts when other people were around. The girls wore dresses most of the time. Most of us wore what we had. Remember, we had two new changes of clothing each year. We sure could have used a thrift store back then, but no one we knew would have had anything to donate.

Extended families often lived next to one another in those days. My grandfather and grandmother, who lived across the street, lived in a nice house. He had worked in the coal mines, and from his example, everyone needed to work long, hard days and be grumpy all the time. Money served as the main driving force my grandfather used to gauge everything by. He always looked at the little money I had and said, "You're never going to buy anything with that."

As a boy, I was thrown into the world of delegated duties quickly. The grade school I attended was a couple miles away. Sometimes I walked to school, and at other times, I rode the bus. (When you were a kid, did anyone ever ask you, Do you ride the bus or carry your lunch? [Bad joke. That was one of our sayings back then.]) When the weather was bad, I walked to the bus stop and took the bus to school. When I got home…oh, yeah, delegated duties. I was expected to pump gas and help in the store.

My grandfather on the other side of the family was totally the opposite of Pops. He did not seem materialistic at all. He had owned a small bakery behind his house, which was one of the smallest houses in the area. He and Grandma had little money. Neither of them had a driver's license or owned a vehicle. They never mentioned money, and material things did not matter much to them. They always seemed to be okay. Their contentment with life was different, and they always made you feel so at home when you visited their house. What made them so different? Stay tuned, and if you are not careful, you might just find out.

The people who lived in our area were pretty friendly for the most part. They settled their own problems, and the churches were quite formal. Pastors and priests seemed way above the rest of us. My grandparents who lived across the street did not ever attend church. My other grandparents lived on the outskirts of a large town about eight miles away. They attended the Greek Orthodox Church. I had no idea at the time what that meant. My parents did not go to church much either, but we kids had to go to Sunday school. We walked there on Sundays regardless of the weather.

Working in the evenings and weekends became a way of life for me. As time went on though, I found out there was a baseball field a little distance from where we lived. I soon got hooked on playing baseball with all the local guys. I later joined a baseball team and made friends with different kids in our league.

When I first experienced playing baseball, we lost every game we played the first half of the season. The two guys who pitched—or tried to pitch—walked just about everyone. One day, our coach saw my cousin and me playing catch. We played a game called Pitcher and Catcher. One of us pitched and the other one caught and called balls and strikes. If you walked a guy, you gave up a run. You pitched until you got three outs. Then you switched places with the catcher, and he did the same. We would go three innings to see who won. The coach watched us and asked, "Have you ever pitched in a game?"

I said, "No, but I'll give it a try."

My cousin did not want to pitch in front of anyone. This would prove to be one of the best ventures I pursued for many years to come. I pitched, and we started winning games. The second year we played in the Little League division, we took first place, and I made the all-star team as a pitcher. Playing our game of Pitcher and Catcher every day paid off.

Many underlying things went on in our area, but I had no clue about them. That was because in those days, no one had phones or electronic devices. Most did not even have newspapers—thank you, Jesus! The people who mentored me had no clue either. Most people were clueless about the forces at work in our area. No one considered the spiritual aspects of life or discussed them, not even the pastors or Sunday school teachers I knew.

Several times in my early years, I saw images in people. It was kind of weird, but I saw dark, black images in people, and bad feelings came to me when I did. I had no idea what they were. I saw them once in a great while. Talk about weird. Boy, was I in for a surprise!

2

The Dad Effect

My dad, who was a very kindhearted man, loved working on vehicles. He told us he had started working on trucks in the Army motor pool. He served as a sergeant in the Korean War. He never talked much about his military experience. When he got out, he started the mechanic garage with his brother.

Dad dedicated himself to his work. He worked seven days a week, and when he finished for the day, he was at home every night. He made sure if I went to him with a problem, he always took the time to explain to me the answer. My dad gave everyone a nickname. Some of them were very unique, and some of the names he came up with fit the person to the tee, and sometimes they were kind of funny. For example, he called two guys Henny and Gummy. He called two other guys Oopdeeduty and Udeejet. My dad's good sense of humor kept us going many times through hard situations.

I spent most of my time working in the small one room, sort of like a small convenience store, at the garage or I was at my grandfather's farm helping out with whatever I could do for my size until I got older. It became a way of life for me. My grandfather, the retired coal miner, always came around Dad's shop to work on something. Because he and I were usually there together, we got to be close for many years. As time went by, things changed. "Some good, some not so good," as John Wayne would say. He also said, "Life is hard, and it's a lot harder if you're stupid." Imagine that.

My Dad worked long, hard days, and each week, he got paid for his work. I always thought the garage belonged to my dad and uncle. Boy, was I ever in for a surprise. The garage, store, and office were all one building, with a small room for the store, a small office, two large bays for repairs, and a large garage-like storage area for trucks, a large wrecker, and other equipment. This turned out to be a good place for my friends and me and to play around and get in trouble with my dad, uncle, and grandpa. At night, it was a great place for us guys to play hide-and-seek. I remember I had a gun that lit up with a bright-red light on the end to show flames from the barrel. I thought it was really cool to this day. It is just one of those guy things.

At the small store in the front of the garage, my dad offered his customers' credit. He put a lot of trust in people. They would buy gas, cigars, or candy or they would charge their repairs or gas purchases and then sign a book that had their names in a little tab. At the end of each month, they were to pay down to zero before any new charges could be made, but that rarely happened. They rarely paid on time or in full. Because Dad was so trusting, he always gave people credit.

Many times, we would get stuck for the charges—mostly by people we knew. It seemed the people with money were usually the ones who did not pay their bills in full. They would leave charges, go, and not pay. This upset Dad, and as times got tough, when work got slow, it got harder to deal with their lack of paying their bills. The circle of life revealed itself in upward and downward spirals over and over through the years. The materialistic values and survival for some families were all they had to hold onto.

My grandfather had an old dog named Duke, who would always lie in everyone's way as they came in and out of the store. Many times, customers tripped over Duke. That was one way you could tell if they had ever been in the store/office before. Duke never moved or got excited about anything. He was a huge, overgrown beagle, probably about fifty pounds overweight. I remember watching every day as my grandpa and Duke walked across the road for lunch in what seemed like a slow-motion pattern.

My grandfather had a farm, and on that farm, he had a cow, and Bingo was his name, oh. (Just kidding. Could not resist.) He really did have a large farm though. Another mystery to me was: Where did he get the money to buy such a large farm?

You might see a pattern starting here, but I was delegated to work on the farm when the need arose, which was more often than not. I thought it was great to be the big guy driving the tractor, but, another but, soon to prevail were the blisters I got on my butt. Asking for a cushion to sit on was out of the question or any sign of weakness that would not be manly. Farming a one hundred plus acre spread was a big task for a small group of part-timers.

One section of the farm was filled with fruit trees ranging from plum to pears to many different types of apples. Another large section was for vegetables of all type to be grown. We had planted thousands of young hemlock and spruce trees on the north side of the farm. Two large ponds on the property were full of catfish and bass. When we threw in chunks of bread, the top of the water turned black with fish.

The farm also had a small spring house that was probably twenty feet deep with cool, crystal-clear water. It remained cool, even when the temperature hit a hundred degrees.

Grandpa hid a string, which he tied in the corner on the inside of the spring house. It led to a stone that ran deep into the water. That was where he hid his beer and liquor from everyone, especially Grandma. One day, we found his stash of beer. He warned us, "Don't you dare tell Grandma!" We did not know how bad Pop's drinking problem was.

I did not know his arthritis and other health problems were what made him very irritable at times. His excessive drinking was his way to ease the pain. Another example of the dark side was prevailing.

I was often put into situations when I was young that as an adult, I would steer clear of. On several occasions, my Mom and grandfather argued violently with each other. My mother was a very reserved woman. I could not imagine what caused her to argue with nearly uncontrollable anger, let alone with, of all people, Grandpa, whom I called Pop.

As the years went by, I saw for myself the buildup of crust that formed. The love of money can change anyone, and that was a big part of the basis for these battles. Battles go on every day, which we do not see—inward spiritual battles. Most people have no clue. They have no clue whatsoever.

I worked in the small office and store with one telephone—the old circle dialer—type, all black telephone with worn out letters, and a bench against the wall next to the door that led to the gas pumps. I could see the gas pumps through the large steel-lined windows. As I watched through the windows, I knew when a car had pulled in for gas; the retired guys hung out telling stories of working in the mines and serving in the war. The stories caught my interest and seemed exciting the first couple times I heard them. After many years of listening though, it was sad to hear the depth of their insight into life—or total lack thereof.

The stories of fishing, trapping lines, and hunting held great interest for a young boy. I always felt a tugging at my spirit as I could somehow see things were definitely missing in some people. It was as if they were shells with no real substance. I hope that makes sense because that was how it felt. I had no idea just what lay in store for me.

The Adventures of Wild Bill—Not Really

As the story progressed, I was riding my bike one morning. I had just been at my cousin's house, and one of the guys on the ball team ran up to me and said, "Hey, did you hear? There was a bad accident on the other side of Main Street. A couple people got killed."

I asked, "Who was it?"

No one knew. My dad drove the local wrecker service from his service station. He towed wrecked vehicles, so he would know. I rode my bike to the garage. Sure enough, Dad knew. It was one of my close friends and his brother. Not a good thing at all. I found it very hard going to a funeral for the first time.

We were a close bunch of guys, and yet, during the funeral visitation, we were kind of lost for what to say. Afterward, I remember taking my bike and following a trail for some distance, then hiking to the top of a mountain and looking out over the valley. It was a beautiful place. I yelled as loud as I could, "Why, God? Why? I don't understand how something like this could happen!" You know, I had the strangest feeling that day: that God heard me. This might seem weird, but I knew that somehow He was listening to me. I walked down the hill and rode my bike home. I felt at peace, and it was as if all the bad stuff that had gone on those couple days was gone.

I had been one of the altar boys and acolytes on rotation at our church. I do not remember the pastor or the church addressing any of the problems going on in our community. It was church on Sunday and then nothing until next week, same time, same station. We met again, and the cycle continued on and on. It was kind of sad.

Again, the forces were at work, but who, what, where, and why was no one asking or searching? In that vacuum, weird groups and witchcraft were everywhere. The spiritual dark side was prevailing in many places. None of us guys understood what those groups stood for or what they did.

3

New Places, New Faces

I attended a small hick town school. Some of the families had it pretty bad in those days. The school nurse even came around once a week to give us all a piece of fruit and a piece of cheese so we would not get sick. A wood and coal stove stood in the corner. It had been used in the recent past to heat the classroom on cold winter days.

The small school was closing. Not many kids attended classes, so some classes were combined. Eventually, we had to merge with the city school about eight to ten miles away. This changed everything for us. We were being bused some place we did not want to go. This town had been our biggest enemy or rivalry in everything we did. No one spoke well about the kids in the town.

My friends and I did not see this as a good thing at all. As kids, we had no say or choice in any of these matters. Even so, we guys thought everything was an adventure. Our first couple of weeks were not so good. The local guys in the school had gangs. They all stuck together and had their clicks.

We entered totally unprepared for this. Fights broke out in the locker rooms and during gym class. Fights happened as some of us walked anywhere alone after school or into the downtown area after school. So many times, fights would break out on the side streets as we walked to events going at the high school either after school or during night games. The high school was about a two-mile walk from the middle school.

The middle school I attended got a new principal. He was a big guy, and in a short time, he made his rounds through all the classes. He put a stop to the gang fights. He also carried a very large paddle, and if you got called to the office, you were guaranteed to feel it. I saw the biggest guys in school return from a visit to the principal with tears in their eyes. (I never got it. Thank God.)

A darkness, an anger-like rage, seemed to fill some of the gang people we encountered from time to time. You could see the underlying spirit of anger and darkness in their eyes. The sad part was you kind of got used to it. That was not good. I had not seen anything like this, and it was a big shock at first. People seemed to harden themselves because they had to survive. They had no other choice.

The churches were hard-core religion. Was there another option, a good spiritual helper? Maybe so. I can look back and see clearly other spiritual forces worked against us. The anger, the fights, the bullies were symptoms.

You could not imagine the hard times some kids endured, the beatings from local kids who knew the area and the ropes. My friends and I had to pull guys off kids who were being beaten and bullied many times. When I made the first string on the JV football team, it seemed the thugs left us sports guys alone for some reason or another. That was okay with me.

Thank God we had enjoyable things to do. Some offered me the opportunity to learn skills I would need in the future. I was at an age when guns were popular, and we had a lot of space in the middle of nowhere on the farm, so we could shoot and hunt.

My grandfather was an expert marksman, and so was my dad. They taught me how to hit unbelievable targets, whether stationary or on the move. We shot nearly every week on the farm. Sometimes I shot every day if I had the chance. We sometimes shot targets from two or three hundred yards using guns with open sites.

Sometimes we shot across the field from a moving truck on a rough road. What great fun! We could purchase ammunition at a very low price. We were fortunate Pop had a sporting goods store at the end of the garage building, which was where we bought most of our ammo.

My dad entered me in shooting competitions against adults when I was just a boy. They seemed easy to me. I came home from them with turkeys, chickens, or other prizes. Mom was always happy to cook up the prizes for supper.

One time, I was in a competition with a guy, and we both kept hitting the bull's-eye, so they set an aspirin pill on a ledge next to the target. We both hit the pill, and it exploded. So they turned the pill on its side. It was all you could do to see the edge of the pill. I thought, *Well, this will separate the men from the boys.* He shot and missed. Now the pressure was on me. I shot, and the pill exploded. Well, I did not have a headache, so I didn't need the aspirin. All this would help me to stay alive in the future.

As the years went by, *the rock just died, Susie went and left me for another guy and…*oops, sorry. Kind of got carried away there again. Couldn't resist.

When I was in high school, my dad became very sick. He spent a long time in the hospital. He was self-employed, but my uncle and grandfather could run the business or so I thought. The bedroom I shared with my brothers was next to my parents' room. By this time, I was the only guy left at home. You see, my brother went off to war, and my other brother tried to hide at college so our Uncle Sam could not find him, and it worked.

A large window had once been in the wall between the bedrooms, and it was covered over with a thin piece of paneling-like material. I heard my mother crying herself to sleep many nights. We had no money coming in to pay for food or to pay the bills. I had a hard time dealing with this. I got into trouble at school. I got into two fights in one day. I had never been in any trouble before at school. The principal was our wrestling coach, and his son was a good friend of mine. I explained what was happening, and he said I should have asked for help.

Other teachers stepped in and helped me a lot. This was a major moment that changed my life. At the time, I did not see it as great as it really was. I was blessed to have teachers who were family-oriented and with good values.

The problem at home was real and did not go away soon. I had to quit my sports activities and work at the garage every chance I got. I still thought the business was my dad's, and people were still getting their cars and trucks fixed, so where was the money going? Everything changed in my life. I was not a kid anymore.

My friends stopped and asked how long I had to work. I had no idea what the future had in store for me. I walked across the street to Pop's house sometimes. They had a television, a color television. I had never seen anything like it before. The first show I ever saw was a baseball game. The grass on the field was bright green. Wow! I had never seen anything like that before; it was amazing.

My grandmother would ask me if I wanted some ice cream. I always said, "Sure!" Who would turn down ice cream? Their house was beautiful inside even though it was not very big. I remember they had a professional painter come in and do some kind of faux painting on the living room and the den. They had a nearly new car. Walking across the street was like walking into a different world from our family life.

One time, Pop said, "We drove to the lake yesterday and picked cherries." They had a whole bushel of sweet red cherries. I was in heaven eating those cherries. Grandma gave me a bowl of cherries to take home. There was no comparison to the way our family lived. This was like a dream world at their house compared to our small apartment.

My uncle lived in an apartment next to us with his family. One day, he said they were going to build a new house. For months, I thought, *It would be the greatest thing in the world to have a new house and a yard to play in.* What an exciting feeling it must have been for them. I thought for some time, *How can they build and afford a new house? He works with my Dad every day.* I couldn't figure it out. Where was everyone getting the money? I had no concept at all. As I look back, we were so dysfunctional. I cannot remember where I got it, but there was this small book, pamphlet-like, that had pictures all though it of new homes. I can still remember some of the pictures of ranch style homes with beautiful landscaping all around the front and sides. All I could do was dream of living in a new, beautiful home like that.

During all those years of disarray, we never once got together as a whole family for anything, not Christmas or anything else. As they say, "Divide and conquer." Whose MO is that?

It seemed the forces that were out there worked on steroids for years to come. The dark side was quite visible at times if you knew where to look. Our church remained the same every Sunday. Everyone sat in the same seats. It was a denominational church.

The different pastors who worked in our church retired and needed a place to rest because they brought no enthusiasm at all to our church. This was purely religion on steroids. I had no clue of how the church could help or where the spiritual forces working in our lives originated.

One night, someone broke into my grandparents' house and stole five thousand dollars in cash. For starters: five thousand dollars? Where was all that cash, and where did they get it? I knew, somehow, I knew who took the money. I could not explain to anyone how I knew, but I could see him as if in a dream taking the money. I mentioned it a couple times, but it fell on deaf ears. Who was showing me who took the money? And those dark, cloud-like images in people from time to time, which I kept seeing, what was that all about anyway?

I worked full time at the garage now. One evening, I was changing tires, and a friend came in and said, "Did you hear about Alan? He hung himself at the car wash last night."

That seemed impossible. Tom, his neighbor, was a close friend of mine. The weekend before, we had just gone to the site where the new school was being built.

I had ridden my motorcycle through the trails to Tom's house. It was about six or seven miles away, and when I got there, Tom, Alan, and a friend said, "Come on, we want to show you what we've been doing."

It was in the evening and dark outside. We walked about five minutes through a patch of woods to the construction site, where they kept all the equipment for clearing and excavating the site for the new high school.

A jeep sat there with a trailer hooked to it. One of the guys unhooked the trailer, and Tom began hot-wiring the jeep. The next thing I knew, it was running. This was crazy. I thought this was happening way too fast.

Tom said, "Get in and hold on!"

I was shocked, to say the least. We flew around the site. This seemed like so much fun, but it was not what I would do.

We could see police lights coming our way. My heart jumped to my throat. Tom whipped the jeep around on a sharp turn, and it went up on two wheels. We all screamed.

Not good. This was not good at all. The jeep nearly tipped over, and we spun around.

Tom yelled, "They'll never catch us!"

He spun the jeep around and headed for a large underground drainpipe where the creek flowed through under the dirt road on the lower end of the construction site.

I thought, *Wow! We are in the clear. They'll never catch us now.*

Suddenly, we could hear a loud screech. The jeep came to a very quick stop. It was wedged in the large cement drainpipe about fifty feet into the pipe underground. Everyone flew into the windshield. Ouch. Good thing none of us got knocked out. We all squeezed out of the jeep and ran out of the drainpipe for the remaining fifty feet or so. We were scared and running for our lives, well, at least I was.

I ran all the way to my motorcycle. It was a small, beat-up Honda trail bike. I hopped on and flew home scared out of my wits. I did not see anything going on with Alan that would make me expect him to take his own life. He had seemed okay. I was dismayed and heartbroken.

New Expeditions

It was the end of summer. We were all in high school now, and there were a lot of hunting camps in our area where someone knew the owners. On the weekends, we would build fires, cook venison, play cards, and sneak beers to drink. Not many of us were of legal age to drink.

One Sunday morning, my brother woke me up and said, "Gordie is dead. They found him lying on a back road. He had been run over with a car or truck."

"No way!" I said, "That's impossible. How could that happen?"

So many weird things were going on in our lives, and yet life continued. No one had any answers, and no one seemed to ask many questions. The dark side was coming out again and again. People had no idea that there was and is a dude called Satan who was having his way in people's lives. No one in specific, but especially me, had a clue about the spiritual side of our lives.

Winter had set in again. One thing was certain: the seasons. The weather got bad in the winter where we lived.

It was always cold with a lot of snow. Hunting season was a winter tradition in our area. If you shot a big buck or a bear or a large turkey gobbler, all the guys knew. Word traveled fast. We had no cell phones, but we did use CB radios or walkie-talkies.

One time, I was supposed to be a hunting guide for some guys from out of state whom Grandpa knew. I wanted to hunt alone until the second week of the season. He said, "Okay, that will work. I'll tell them next week."

The next day, it was around fifteen degrees outside with strong gusts of wind. That was good. The deer could not hear me moving, and my scent would be scattered. I set out about 4:30 a.m. I had walked about two or three hours out through the valley and into a mountainous part of the region when snow began to fall quite heavily.

I watched for deer and thought the area would be easy to navigate. I had been in this area before, but it wasn't wintertime. Now the conditions were getting bad. The heavy snow covered my tracks. I had walked a lot farther and crossed too many valleys to know my direction. I had traveled farther in both distance and time than I thought.

I saw a couple herds of deer. They kept climbing the hills and stayed out in front of me. They stayed just far enough ahead of me that I could not see whether any were bucks.

The day was passing quickly. I did not realize how late it was. I thought, *I better find somewhere out of this storm soon before night sets in.*

I walked down the side of one of the mountains and found a large hemlock tree. I had my hunting knife strapped to my belt. I started carving notches in some large branches from the hemlock so I could break them off. After breaking off a bunch of branches, I made a tepee-like area where I could sit. Then I lined the bottom with several layers of branches with the heavy needles facing up so I could curl up in them and spend the night. I laid my gun beside me and curled up inside for a long, cold night.

I said a prayer, knowing God knew where I was on this cold, snowy night in the middle of thousands of acres of woods. I could not hear a sound outside, and nothing distracted me. God knew my heart, and that night, as all the other nights, He was with me. It was a good thing because I needed His protection.

The next morning, I woke up. The snow had stopped. Thank God for that. About a foot of fresh snow had fallen on top of the snow we already had. I climbed out of the tent. The only thing I had to eat was a scrunched up Milky Way bar. I made the mistake of eating it so fast I did not even taste it.

I was so run down from all the hiking the day before and not eating or drinking anything that the candy bar did not quite agree with me, if you know what I mean.

I knew I had to find a way out soon. I did not want to spend another night out there without being prepared. I thought, *What are my options?* Okay. Survival tips: While lost in the deep forest, I had not come across a large stream or road all day yesterday.

I thought I must be south of the main mining area where I came in. I climbed to the highest point I could find and still saw no sign of civilization at all. I heard no distinct noises that would guide me out or to someone. I counted my ammo, and I had eighteen rounds. I thought, *Fire three shots in the air, then wait.* I did just that. I waited. Nothing.

About forty-five minutes passed, and I thought, *I'll climb up the next hill,* which was about an hour walk, and I fired three more shots. I waited. I only had twelve or thirteen rounds left. About five minutes passed, and I heard a shot from about a half a mile away. I fired three more shots to show my location and waited.

Sure enough, after about an hour's wait, I could see someone off in the distance hiking up the valley at a fast pace. As he walked closer to the hillside where I was, I waved so he could see me.

I wore a bright, florescent-orange hat and vest, and so did he. It was buck season, so you needed to wear orange to be visible. The hunter walked up to me and said, "I heard your distress shots the first time but couldn't get a bearing on exactly where you were until you moved up higher and fired again." We talked for quite a while, and I told him how I had spent the night out here last night. I asked him where I was on the map and how to get out of there. He said I would have to walk about another hour and a half and follow the two large ridges to get to a main road, which was about thirty miles from where I had started. I told him "thanks." We shook hands, and off I went. Talk about guardian angels! This guy was there for a reason.

When I found the road and a place with a pay phone—yes, a pay phone—I called one of my buddies for a ride back to my jeep. My guardian angel sure worked overtime on that journey. Thank you, Jesus. As you can see, God uses people in our lives. I was not missed much yet because sometimes during hunting season, I would stay at the farm in the trailer.

Meanwhile, back at the ranch, the work had started on my uncle's house. The excavating had started. It was being built next to the garage. I thought, *Wow! How could this be? It's my dad's property.* Again, no one said anything or asked any questions. There was always a weird sense of "It is okay. Keep doing what you're doing, and it will all work out. Just do not ask." My dad was still not allowed to work. It looked like his health was to the point he would not get back to work. He tried several times but could not handle the physical aspects of his job or any stress.

Medical treatment was poor in those days, especially where we lived. I always thought, *Dad, run the business and let other people do the physical work.* That never happened. It did not make sense to me at all.

I had tried several times to get my dad to walk away from the garage so he and I could start our own business, but he was not able to start over at that point. I said, "Dad, we can do this together."

He said, "It's okay. Things will work out."

As John Wayne said, "Right will prevail, Henry, right will prevail."

Well, it sure did not seem that way, at least for the time being.

This would turn out to be, which I had no clue for many years, something that would bring a turn of many events in my life that would bring the dark side prevailing over and over again.

One night, I was riding my small Honda 90 motorcycle. It was an old trail bike. I spent a lot of time taking it apart and rebuilding it with what I had. It ran well. Off I went over the mountains and the back, dirt roads. It had a small headlight that was not too bright, just like some of the people I knew, oops.

I could not fathom how I could ride all that distance with very little candle power on those paths or back roads in the middle of the night in the middle of nowhere. Someone rode with me every time. I thought, *Why drive all the way around?* It was four or five miles that way. Why not take a shortcut? (Shortcuts have never and I mean never worked out for me). The power line had a trail, and it was probably less than half the distance and more fun going that way, so I thought, *Why not?*

I turned off onto the trail and had gone about halfway when I came over the mountaintop and started down the other side. I could see what appeared to be a light of some kind off in the distance. As I got closer, my small headlight barely lit the trail in front of me. I was in a hurry and trying to get home—it was getting late—and not paying much attention, but as I got closer, it became apparent the light I was seeing was a large fire.

People gathered all around the fire. They all had white sheets pulled over themselves. A wooden cross, which was painted white, stood next to the fire. This happened so fast; I found it hard to fathom it all.

The really scary part expas they could see me, but I couldn't see who any of them were. As I got closer, some of the people saw me coming because of my headlight. They ran toward me. Not good. I gave that little bike all it had, which was not much.

They all stood in a field, so for my benefit, I drove quickly around everything and stayed on the trail. I headed home on the back roads, scared out of my wits. I was scratched up pretty good from all the briars I drove through late last night.

This started a series of bad situations for me. During that time, I had no clue how to see the connection between the people under the masks and things to come. Some of the people under the masks turned out to be some prominent people in the area.

In our area, if you saw someone, you recognized him, but you might not know all of them by name. Given that degree of acquaintance, it was hard to see how much that went on—including witchcraft, sorcery, and Ku Klux Klan activities—were practiced and believed. Yet no one talked about them openly. This scenario was the same in many small towns across our country. For example, years later, I found out the leader of the KKK lived just a short distance from us. Talk about weird.

As we returned to our families and ongoing lives, my family was struggling. My uncle's family was thriving. My grandparents were living the dream. That remained a mystery to me. As time passed, my dad worked out a deal with an old, retired gentleman who had a vacant piece of property he wanted to get rid of. He practically gave it to us.

A large mine had been located on the property. It was now abandoned and in disarray. An old house-type camp stood on the edge of the property. I had found a part-time job working for a local contractor who tore down old commercial buildings. Over several months of working for him, the owner had given me used materials, windows, doors, or whatever to barter with me for the work I had done. I thought, *Great! This is another perfect situation that didn't just happen by chance.* Again, the spiritual forces out there work with you or against you.

Other guys also brought materials so we could make the old house-like camp livable and eventually turn it into a house someday. Maybe my parents could even live there.

The property was about two miles from the garage. Pop and I helped put a new roof on the house. When I climbed up on the two-story roof, I was a little leery at first of being up that high. My uncle teased me about being scared of heights.

The love of money and greed were the driving force in the outcome of things that followed. One afternoon, no one knew where Pop had been all day. Had he been at the farm working or was he in the back of the garage working? No one knew, but after several hours of looking everywhere, someone yelled, "I found him!"

He had been working on the flat roof of the third story of the garage roof above where the wrecker was stored at. He had a heart attack on the roof and was lying there face up. He had died early in the afternoon.

This left my grandma who had kept the books for the garage to manage things. She threw in the towel and said it was too much. Upon Pop's death, everything came out.

My grandfather had the garage and property in his name. The money from the business was hidden in CDs in his name in another bank. He had about eighty or ninety thousand dollars in CDs. This might not seem like much now, but where we lived many years ago, it was a lot of money.

Looking at the greed and how Pop had lived for himself all those years were very hard on our family. My mother had known all along what was going on, but my dad would not stand up and go against his father. Kind of sad if you give it some real thought though.

That was why my mother had been so angry with my grandfather. We never prayed and looked to God or Jesus for answers or help. Life just kept rolling along.

They say life is like a roll of toilet paper. At first, the roll is big, and it goes down very slow. The same as your life; when you are young, the years go by slowly. Then as the roll gets smaller, look how fast it disappears. The same with your life; as you get older, the years go by faster and faster. Maybe it is not the best analogy, but it works.

The year after I graduated from high school, my uncle operated the garage on his own. He did minor repairs. This was a big change from seeing everyone working and the place buzzing with people.

I had found a job in a small machine shop because it was time to move on and get a real job.

I had still been playing baseball with all the guys in the neighborhood every chance we got. Playing baseball was my favorite thing to do. I had made the decision to travel for an all-star team across the state. It was hard trying to work, pay bills, and still have time to play ball and go on the road to play when needed.

One evening in August, I went fishing. I was back up in the mountains and had parked my jeep off the road next to a drainage pipe, a large cement pipe under the road. I loved to fish and still do to this day. I had caught a couple nice trout on the small steam that ran through the hills and into the reservoir. It was getting dark, so I packed it in and went home.

That evening, I went to the local club where all the guys hung out, drank beer, and shot shuffleboard. There was a card table where a lot of the guys played card games all evening. Two of the guys I knew came up to me. I thought I knew them quite well, and they were angry. One of them said to me, "What's the big idea going out there today and messing with our stuff?"

I had no clue what they were talking about. It turned into a pushing and shoving match that was broken up by my friend Mike.

After they left, Mike came up to me and said, "Do you know why they're so ticked off?"

I said, "No."

He went on to explain they had a ton of marijuana plants growing all around the springs and tunnels up there.

These were also the same guys who stole the money from my grandparents, which was my dad's money from his business. I could not prove anything. (Several years later, one of these guys committed suicide by overdose over his girlfriend.)

If only we had a good church where we could have turned, we could have turned these situations around. It might have been different. In the Apostle Paul's life at the church in Ephesus, he dealt with similar problems among the believers there. This is so sad because we have a God who is alive and waiting for us to acknowledge Him.

Many evil spiritual strongholds exist in certain areas of our country, but good people have no spiritual knowledge to turn to for strength and a faith in Jesus. I have to say it again; a good, honest, and Holy Spirit–filled church would put to flight these battles by Satan. This would be the solution to even these situations.

5

Opportunities—Some Good, Some Not So Good

I applied for a job as a machinist's helper and was surprised I passed the test and got the job. I purchased all my tools and the study books needed to work with a senior tool and die maker. It was a very different experience. I had to always give my 100 percent focus to my work. I could have no outside thoughts or I would lose concentration on the processes and calculations I worked through. It was a very hard process, but I was up for the challenges. I finished the program in a couple of years, thank God for that.

The company owner's son went through the program the same time I did. He proved to be spoiled-rotten and was also into everything illegal. Because of that, I needed to get a different place of employment soon. I started searching for a job with a different company so I could advance my skills even more.

One day, while I was driving back from fishing, I decided to stop at a local ice cream shop to have my favorite: a hot fudge sundae. I noticed what looked like a factory next to the ice cream shop. I walked across the lot and saw a sign that read "Office." I entered the office and asked if they were hiring. The receptionist told me they were not. I asked to fill out an application anyway. She said that would be okay and that they would keep my application on file. I told her "thanks" and headed out.

The ice cream tasted exceptionally good that day, so good I went out of my way to stop there again the next day. It really was not just the ice cream though that made the day bright. I was ready to order the same hot fudge sundae, the best dessert on the planet, even better than apple pie. They should change the slogan from "baseball, hot dogs, and apple pie" to "baseball, hot dogs, and hot fudge sundaes!"

Someone was watching out for me again, but who? As I waited my turn to order, a voice yelled, "Hey, are you buying?"

I gave the right answer, "Sure."

It was the owner of the factory. He was a big guy, bald, and kind of stocky—a jolly old elf. (Sorry, could not resist.)

He said, "I saw you here yesterday, and I looked over your application."

We finished our sundaes, and he said, "Can you come over to the shop tomorrow around noon?"

I said, "Sure, I will be here."

Something seemed different about this guy and in a good way. It seemed as if we were old friends. The next day, Mr. Phil showed me around the shop.

Someone said, "Hey, Five Pin."

I looked around, and a man named Ben, an older guy, was running a special diamond sharpening machine.

He was grinning, and he said, "Old Five Pin there is sitting, doing nothing again."

I didn't know at the time, but these guys were all on a bowling team, and Jack always missed the five pin. That was how he got his nickname.

Mr. Phil said, "Hey, it's lunchtime!"

So everyone went to the lunchroom for their half-hour lunch break. Everyone was pretty much finished with lunch, and their half hour was about up, but the boss, Mr. Phil, came back in and said, "Hey, where's everyone going? Let's play cards."

You see, Mr. Phil loved playing cards, and he enjoyed hanging out with the guys even more.

They said to me, "Hey, young man. Come on, sit in, and play a game of cinch."

I said, "Sure, why not?"

We played a couple games, and everyone went back to work. What a different place. They seemed to be a close bunch of guys who enjoyed working together.

Mr. Phil said, "Hey, we start at seven in the morning. Do you want the job?"

I thought, *Wow! Working here and the training to do it, what a great opportunity.* I shook his hand and said, "Thank you very much."

He grinned, patted me on the back, and said, "See you tomorrow morning at seven o'clock sharp—and don't be late."

I soon learned that was one of his many favorite sayings.

Time went by fast there. Those several years of work and training were a good experience. I got to be close friends with the guys. I can see now how much I needed a family environment even at work. The work experiences, training, and friendships were priceless. The machine training, heat treating, and tooling work were tough experiences but would prove to be worth it over time.

We built parts for prototype airplanes, helicopters, and experimental aircraft. We worked on a lot of high-tech stuff. Mr. Phil was a great guy and a terrific boss. Mr. Phil was retiring soon and leaving the business to his son, Ben, who had the nickname Never Sweat because Phil said Ben never worked a hard day in his life.

Things started to change a lot and not for the better. He was right about Never Sweat.

Another year went by, and it seemed I was spending way too much time drinking with my buddies and hanging out at the club after work. I was not doing so well in my personal life. I had no one to turn to for any guidance. My days seemed to blend together one after another, and my only hope was my work. Drinking made my problems worse.

I lived on the corner of my cousin's property. He said I could fix it up as payment on the place. The neighbor who lived a couple houses up from me, I had worked on his car a couple of times in my garage. I was repairing cars and painting some cars and motorcycles in my garage too.

I got so busy that the days turned into months. Once, after working on my neighbor's sports car, he told me the place where he worked was hiring. It was a huge factory.

He told me to use him as a reference because he knew the owners. I told him, "Thanks."

Once again, that Someone was watching over me, no matter how I messed things up in my life.

I went to the factory the next day and put in an application for employment in the engineering department. After I filled out my application, the secretary said, "That's a very difficult department to get into." She told me to check back the next Tuesday, and she would update my application and let me know of any changes.

I never missed a Tuesday for more than six months.

One Tuesday afternoon, I was in the office updating my application for the twentieth time when the secretary said, "You are very persistent, and you haven't missed a week in updating your application for a long time. One of the company's owners was walking through the office when the secretary said, "Mr. Bob, this is the gentleman I told you about."

He shook my hand and said, "You have a good reputation around here already. You haven't missed a week for more than six months now."

He told the secretary to pull my file. She said, "I already have it right here."

"You seem like you want a job working for us pretty bad," he said.

"Yes, sir, I do," I said.

He said, "I will give you a chance. Do not let me down."

I said, "Thank you, sir. I won't."

I got a job working in the shop in the machining and engineering department. I worked with the factory's engineers.

As time went by, I got to be friends with some of the engineers and the maintenance crews.

No one really spoke a lot while working or even during breaks. I kept quiet and listened to the older engineers when they talked. I did not impose on any private conversations. The English was broken and hard to understand when some of them talked. I was patient, and after a while, I understood their lingo.

If these guys did not trust you, they would tell you. Then they banished you, just like that. We worked twelve-hour days and long weeks sometimes on special projects. It turned out most of the people I worked with were from Russia and Germany. That explained their broken English.

Mr. Schmidt told me he had to change his name when he got here so no one would find him. A couple of other guys were in the same situation; they were there because they needed to change location. These guys were outstanding engineers. Some of the things we designed and built were amazing.

After a while, we got to be good friends.

One evening, as we walked down one of the long old corridors, Mr. Von told me, "There are microphones all through here and hidden cameras."

I said, "No way! Why would they do that?"

He whispered to me, "If we go through those doors, I will show you."

Just then, stepping out from out of nowhere, stood big Al, the security chief. He looked like a bad guy from a James Bond movie. "Where are you guys going?

"Uh, nowhere, Al, we were just eating our lunch."

The entire factory was secure, and you needed a security clearance badge to get into our work area.

I did not realize the area where I worked was off limits to everyone except our department. We worked on advanced technology for the military and other special automotive projects.

Some of the guys from Russia invited me to their homes on several occasions. You would not believe the homes they had built. One family lived in a log cabin. It was rustic but beautiful. You could see no electrical wires from outside sources, yet they had running water, lamps, and a refrigerator.

They had dug a small pond just below the front yard. It had a small stream running through it. The pressure from the water on the bottom of the pond fed a pipe up the hill through the yard to the house to an underground tank and then to the faucets. The force from the pressure and gravity in the pond meant no pump or electricity was necessary.

What an engineering feat! It was amazing—and it worked. Several paddle wheels operated in the stream and one on the spillway. They produced power for their electricity. This was only a couple of the many features built into the home.

They had also built a diesel train and rail system all through the woods. It looped through the property. When I rode the train, I was amazed once again. What amazed me most was how smoothly the train ran and the perfection in all their work. I was not sure the scale of the train, but it seemed to be about one-third the size of a regular train and cars.

They were a very close family. I made connections with them that lasted a long time. I noticed they had several Bibles in their home. You could see and feel the peace and contentment they lived. What a difference from the world I usually experienced.

I had no idea these guys were being watched closely, and soon, I would be too. This was the start of a stream of circumstances that opened doors—good ones and not so good ones—through all the many years that filled me with regret. Eventually, government agents made their way into my life, and I found no way to get away from their so-called deals.

As I look back, I see the not-so-much coincidence of happenings in my life. I was in junior high, and we were being bused to a neighboring city, and as I'd said before, the gang leaders, alias bullies, were beating up someone in the shower one day after gym class. I walked in and started pulling two guys off Ed who was the kid who always had the pocket pen holder in his button-down shirt pocket and full of lead pencils and pens.

He was bleeding and kind of dazed.

They said to me, "You do not know who you are dealing with."

Well, the big guy always has your back. You see, the super who was in charge of the entire engineering department came one day just about the end of our lunch break.

He sat down beside me, and all eyes and ears in the shop seemed like we had their attention. He put out his hand and said, "Thank you for helping my son."

I said, "You're welcome," but I had no idea what I did.

He went on telling me about how I pulled the guys off his son who were punching and kicking him after gym in the shower room and stood up for him many times afterward.

As winter started to roll in that year, one of my friends who worked with Five Pin said, "Hey, would you be interested in joining our bowling league? We are short one guy. Would you be interested?"

I thought for a minute and said, "Sure, why not? Sounds like fun."

After a couple months of bowling, I was caught up in a team that wanted to be in the finals for the Christmas tournament. I had not expected that. I was a bowl-for-fun guy, and that was where I was when I was driven by the team to change my attitude to "We've got to win this."

Some of the guys were from the place I worked for. They were a good bunch of guys. We bowled for the play-offs and headed into the semifinals of the Christmas tournament. One of the players on the other team was a huge Italian guy. The last time I saw someone who looked like him, it was on WWF (World Wrestling Federation). He looked as if he was not in a good mood.

Ben, the captain of our team, leaned over to me and said, "Do not mess with that guy. He is a pay-for-hire guy."

I asked, "What do you mean?"

Ben had been drinking a lot, and the more he drank, the more he talked. The talking got louder and louder, which was not good. He went on to say, "This guy, Mr. Big, torches places and 'removes' people. So you don't want to mess with him."

I said, "Ben, I don't need to know anymore."

The guy overheard Ben several times and made it clear when he looked at me that he meant business. Remember, I thought this was a fun bowling league. We went on to take third place in the tournament, which was unbelievable in and of itself. I was just glad to get out of there that night.

Several times, when I picked up supplies in the valley, a town about eight miles from our farm, Mr. Big showed up and made sure he walked in and out of the stores where I shopped. Talk about Satan breathing and looking at you in real life! This was not good. It was like watching a movie and then having the characters became real, breathing and moving about. I guess it might depend on the kind of movie—a thriller or a horror movie. I was not sure at that point. Was he one of the guys under those white sheets?

Ben had told me how Mr. Big had torched a local restaurant. They were now building a new one with the insurance money. This was truly like something out of one of those Saturday, late-night mystery movies. I had to get back home and get ready for my afternoon class. I had been late yesterday. I had better get moving or I would be late again.

I was spending a lot of time at the gym at the time. I was one of the instructors. The gym was kind of old-fashioned. One of the guys in my class was a big kid, at least six foot and six inches tall. He was also very good at hand-to-hand combat, which was the focus of our class. I could write a book on the tournaments I was invited to all over the US and some in other countries.

One weekend, they held a mountain man competition at a bar-restaurant located in the mountain section of a small town about thirty miles away. People came from everywhere to compete and watch. Matt, who was the tall kid from the hand-to-hand combat class, was competing. He kept trying to get me to compete, but I said, "You have to be crazy."

Some of the guys looked like they had not seen civilization for quite a while. You had to have the attitude to want to punish the guy in the in the ring you were fighting.

The drinking and fighting were not a pretty sight. It was plain to see how some people enjoyed the violence and blood being shed.

I was glad Matt lost in the early rounds. He got beaten up pretty bad. I left before the last fight of the finals. I had a bad feeling in my stomach that kept telling me: This is not good.

God was tugging at my heart again and again, but I was not listening. A spiritual battle continued inside of me. I could not see it, but it was definitely there. Men often feel that to be successful, they must be the best at something or take charge. That is okay. We need men who are men, but as spiritual leaders, we are short of good men. During that time, none of those guys knew what it meant to be spiritual leaders. Not much had changed since then.

Another large restaurant, about eight miles away from where I lived, burned down one night. No one knew how it started. Rumor had it some people knew. As for me, I kept as far away from Mr. Big and his associates as I could.

6

What Kind of Sport?

One of the friends I worked with for a short time got licensed to be a gun dealer. A bunch of us thought, *Great! Why don't we buy some rifles like M16s or M1As or semi-automatics? That would be a lot of fun.* I had a bunch of machines in my garage, so I thought, *Why don't we make the parts to shoot faster too? That would be great,* so Manny and I did just that. What fun!

We bought a thousand rounds of ammunition at a time, including tracer rounds, so when we shot at night, we could see the fire line. We always shot out in the mountains where it was much safer, and no one was around.

One place was an old dump that had not been used for a long time. We bought thirty and forty shot banana clips for each gun. One of the cool things to do that was like watching Rambo movie; we shot down small trees with bullets. We thought it was cool—like watching Rambo. "You know you drew first blood."

One day, I was on my way home from work; and as always, I kept my CB radio on channel 14, the channel we all used to talk to one another when we were out and about.

The area we messed around in was filled with thousands and thousands of acres of woods, and if you got stuck or broke down, chances were you were on your own.

I heard someone say, "We're in trouble," and they cut off just like that. It sounded like TJ, but I was not sure. There was silence, so I called back, but no one answered. I rode up to the sporting goods store on the edge of main street later, and everyone was frantic.

I said, "What's up?"

A couple of the guys, including Manny, had flipped their guns over to full auto and were shooting rats at the dump. A woman who lived in a trailer on the next hill overheard the shooting and called the police.

Where we lived, you could go a month or two without seeing a police car. We had no local police force. The police came, and because of the automatic weapons, so did the FBI. We panicked, took our guns apart, and dismantled them immediately. Within a couple days, I traded mine for a hunting rifle, probably too hasty a decision but for the best in the end.

For a small town in the middle of nowhere, we sure experienced a lot of craziness. Again, what you see with your eyes and what is going on spiritually can be another world entirely.

My friend Manny, the gun dealer, had just bought an elephant gun—that's right, an elephant gun. The bullets looked bigger than a .50 caliber, so off we went. It was crazy, yes, first, to purchase it and, second, even to suggest shooting it.

But off we went up to where they used to test jet engines secretly around the time of the end of World War II. The site had large cement pillars everywhere, with railroad tracks leading up to them. They were used to test the thrust of jet engines for planes and missiles. We had brought a couple other rifles to shoot in addition to the elephant gun. I shot a couple rounds, as did everyone else, to see the size of the holes or nicks the bullets would make in the cement pillars. Our rounds were nothing when compared to Manny shooting his elephant gun.

He weighed 240–260 pounds and was all muscle, but when he shot the elephant gun, it kicked him like a mule. The next shooter, Fran, was knocked back quite a bit.

When Manny handed me the gun, I thought, *Well, here goes the farm.* I shot, and all I could remember was my ears ringing like a bomb went off and a mule kicked me in the head. Fran and I always arm wrestled, and when we did, the outcome went either way. Neither of us would admit we were the lesser, good friends, guy stuff. In these days, I think I spent more time in my basement and at the "Y" working out and lifting weights more than anything else.

The hole the elephant gun left in the cement was bigger than all the other shots combined. Who would ever buy an elephant gun? Only one of us. You never know, maybe someday, a stampede of wild elephants might come through, and you could save your entire family. Great.

We got back in the jeep and took off.

One of the guys said, "Remember back when we were in junior high and we were camping out and had the bright idea to take our bikes out at night over to the big valley with the hidden pass?"

I said, "Remember that night when we hid our bikes and walked for hours around the hills and climbed over the fence and down the valley until we could see the dirt road that went up the valley?"

We sat there for a while and decided to go back when we heard a faint hornlike sound, and a set of lights came on in the valley.

You could see trucks coming up the road one after another. They just kept coming up the valley and disappearing into the hillside. We tried to get closer, but we could see people walking along the road, and after about thirty minutes, everyone was gone. It got quiet again, so we decided it was time to get out of there. That was a good thing.

We never found out for sure what was in there, but it must have been important. Again, what you see or do not see in people or things might not be what is really going on.

You have probably heard the old saying: "You become like the friends you hang out with." Well, it seems like the weirdness comes out in everyone sooner or later.

One weekend, I was playing in a racquetball tournament with some of the guys from the school where I had been working. I was just playing for fun, but it turned out that was not the case for everyone. Somehow, I managed to make it to the tournament's semifinals; that was very hard to believe.

We were at the new renovated building that used to be a middle school building and renovated by my friend Moose into a health sports complex. There were large glass windows that surrounded the top of the main court so spectators could watch the matches.

I was in the locker room getting ready for my match when a friend came in and said, "You're not going to believe who you're playing."

I thought, *What difference does it make?*

He told me I was playing the judge and added, "He hates to lose."

I thought nothing of it. It was just a game. I played my best all the time, gave it 100 percent, but was just having fun. *Oh, well, here it goes.*

I remember my dad had seen my attitude and the results it produced when I was growing up and he would say, "You're the best!"

We proceeded to play. According to the rules of racquetball, you play to fifteen and must win by two points. The score was thirteen to four. I was not winning and was not paying much attention to the score.

Everyone watched the match from the top floor through the large windows. I thought, *There's no way I am going to let this old guy beat me.* I poured it on and tied the score fourteen to fourteen. The judge was serving and scored the next point. He yelled "yah!" and raised his hand and yelled again, "Game point."

I said, "I don't think so. You have to win by two."

He was not happy, to say the least. He smacked his racket off the floor and said, "Let's go!"

We went back and forth, scoring until we reached eighteen points each.

I thought, *I've had enough. I've got to win this.* I was serving. I scored the next two points and won—or did I? I lost in the long run. As I look back, I lost greatly.

The judge hit his racket on the floor and broke it. He was mad!

I went to the locker room, and my friends came running in and said, "Are you nuts? Beating the judge. You better watch out."

I could hear the judge slam his locker a couple rows over. "This is not over!" he yelled.

How's the song go? "The judge in the town got blood stains on his hands."

I thought, *Wow! What a problem this guy has.* I forgot about it and went to play in the championship. Where did the judge's anger originate? The rage and hatred coming from his spiritual depths was not godly; that was for sure.

He was one of the men under the white sheets leading the groups around the fire in the field in the mountains that night and many others. What were the ramifications? This guy had a lot of power, and he was not afraid to use it to his advantage and purpose.

My life had been a total wreck for years. I did not know it at the time, but I had spirits—not the good ones—in me, controlling my emotions and making my life a living hell. It is hard to change your life when the people around you are weird and the people you look up to are weirder. Who do you turn to when there is no one to turn to? The song with the lyrics "the judge in the town got blood stains on his hands," I think that song originated in our small town. The government surely knew what they were doing by having hidden operations in our area.

Everyone seemed to be too weird in their own ways to see anything extraordinary going on outside of their own lives.

Good place to make a movie—horror movie, that is.

Agents who worked for the government lived in our area for as long as I could remember. At the time, none of us knew who they were. Some of the other guys or thugs who came into my dad's garage for a while and were always hanging around were among them, but at the time, it all seemed normal to us.

I had worked in my own garage for some time over the years. I had built on to the garage several times with my friends' help. We had worked for different manufacturers and specialty companies. I traveled all over the eastern US trying to piece together used machines to run a company that could do versatile work. With those experiences, adding on to my garage was a simple matter.

I remember clearly saying one day, "God, I do not know what I am doing here, but I know if You supply me with work, I will give jobs to those who need work and who can't get other companies to hire them." He was definitely listening again, as always.

I had seen this every day growing up, hearing people say, "Why won't anyone hire me or give me a chance to work to prove myself?"

We went from small machines to computerized machines of all types and designs. We built machines engineers said were impossible to build. I bought many different types of machines and inspection equipment over several years.

We had to have a quality control manual written and inspected soon to qualify our company to be accepted to work for working for companies like Caterpillar or Porter-Cable or Federal-Mogul. I took on that process and had the luxury of having some help from a friend who ran the SPC (Statistical Process Control) department at another factory in our area. After about six months of research and tabulating, I finished the QA 9000 manual for the company. Having all the machines from different type of companies and trying to interface them were impossible for this era in technology. This would put us in a very unique position in our industry.

One thing that made us successful was we interfaced all our equipment so we could tabulate information to store and use for process control data. We also interfaced all our inspection equipment to one computer for storage of data to use for quality control and developed a process to train employees on using the data for the specific work they performed. This is called Statistical Process Control or better known as SPC.

This improved our work and training by a 1,000 percent.

I started a work performance program for all employees based on a monthly report for each employee. This put us ten years ahead of our competition. Miracles do happen. God was at work, and to be honest, I was not aware at the time.

I formed a quality control team of employees and trained them to run the system and showed them how to manage the flow of information.

We proceeded with success to interface all our computerized machines with all the inspection equipment and tied into an SPC computer. Here was the impossible task: No one I knew had ever done that before with all the different types of computer language.

This was the beginning of setting us apart from any other manufacturer our size. Major businesses such as GM or Caterpillar had similar systems that cost millions of dollars to set up in their processes. They most likely had the same types of equipment throughout their shops.

This separated the men from the boys. We restructured again and qualified our process with all our major companies.

To meet the necessary requirements, we had to have a quality control manual to show our process was capable of producing quality work on a consistent basis. Moreover, we had to show we could track our mistakes and show we would not repeat them. This kept us in the running on all the major technical work that was the cutting edge of the industry.

I remember struggling with being competitive when we had to run production runs for a specific part we qualified to make. Somehow, we always came up with good ideas for different processes we needed to be successful. Again, Someone was watching over me.

After hundreds of hours of research and looking at what the competition in Germany and Japan were doing with their competitive manufacturing skills, I decided to take all our production machines and SPC inspection gauges and make work cells for each division of our company. I implemented a profit-sharing plan for all employees based on their work performance. I also implemented a quality control and material process system.

Within a couple of months of training and procedure adjustments, we were off and running like never before. Employees were doubling their salaries, and production went through the roof with quality work. The Big Guy was working overtime. He definitely helped me along with all this. I had no clue that the power of Jesus was so strong and tied into everyone's lives.

We did work for GM, Caterpillar, Porter-Cable, and many other manufacturers. We received some work for the government that seemed impossible to build. But again, that driving spiritual force inside me was always helping make decisions easy for me. I was not always listening well. I was always struggling personally, but it seemed like Someone or something was always protecting me. *Does this happen to everyone?* I wondered. Was this spiritual or what?

7

Guardian (What?)

A major turning point came in my life. It took many years for me to recover from it, and my recollection of what happened was very hard for many years to come. I kind of remember I was walking on a construction job when I was knocked unconscious by a machine and was nearly left for dead. I was life-flighted to a hospital and pronounced dead twice. Somehow, I survived this ordeal and lived to tell about it.

It took many years to remember what happened and to get a grip on a different life. I know now I was a different person then than I am now. I struggled to keep things going at the factory. I had little to no recollection of much of anything for about two to three months. I had a very hard time. I had tremendous headaches and was banged up badly. Gradually, over many years, things came back to me. I do not know quite how to explain it.

I did not have the interest to struggle to grasp the things I was missing. I look back and see I was and am thickheaded at times, and I surely felt pain both physically and spiritually. I believe everyone has a guardian angel who watches over us. My guardian angel surely has a full-time job.

I had gone to a church with a friend of mine, and the pastor said, "We are looking for volunteers to go to South America to do a building project."

I thought, *Great! Why not? I am not getting anything done in my condition. This would be great.* That thought was one the old me would not have ever considered.

We got together for a weekend retreat before leaving on our mission trip. We stayed in tents at a nearby church camp. The lead pastor came into the tent and said it was around eleven o'clock in the morning. Everyone had been up for four or five hours. He tried several times to wake me, but I would not wake up. They let me sleep until late afternoon. Several people tried to wake me again but to no avail.

Early that evening, the pastor tried desperately to get me awake. He said he was going to pour a bucket of water on me next. He knew the trauma my body went through and probably was one of the reasons why he left me to rest.

When I finally woke up, I did not realize how exhausted I had been from the injuries. I guess sometimes we just keep moving and do not take time to replenish our bodies. I would find out in the future that replenishing your spirit is even more important.

I got my things together and packed up for three weeks of working with a large crew of guys from all over the US. We were told to bring tools and clothes with us that we would leave for the church to use when we were done, so I did just that.

A medical team of doctors and dentists were to tag along with us. We were told to go around to all the pharmacies and doctors we knew in our area to see whether they had any outdated medicines they could donate to the trip.

I ended up with a suitcase full of medicine to take. I think we had about eight suitcases full of medicine in all for the doctors and dentists to use on the patients they served while we were there. It's sad to say we cannot do this now.

It seemed that information somehow traveled through channels even back then. I was told by a so-called agent to deliver a Manila envelope to a location in South America, which was where we were headed. "'Someone' will meet you. Give them the envelope," I was told.

This was not good in any shape or form. I had no choice in the matter. I guess I was so tired from everything that I just went along with the crap. I packed it with my suitcase and forgot about it.

We left Miami airport and flew to Dallas where we were to catch another flight to Paraguay.

We were all surprised to see the plane we had to board. It looked like something out of a World War II movie. It had propeller engines on both wings, and most of the windows were cracked. We started our flight, and it was a good thing the weather was good and hot because there was no air conditioning. The seats were all metal, and everything else was metal too. The noise level was so high you had to yell to the person next to you to do any talking at all. It looked like an old military plane from the fifties or sixties.

During the flight, we walked up front to talk to the pilot who was sitting out in the open in front of us with a copilot next to him. We asked him why we were flying so low over the ocean. We could see the waves only several hundred feet below us.

He said that with all the people and supplies, this was all the altitude the plane could get.

Great! Not the kind of answer you would want to hear. This was a great time to pray for some help on getting us safely to our destination.

We needed other wings to help that heap fly that day. This was the start of a trip that would prove to be inspirational, rewarding, and dangerous.

After a long flight, we could see the airport in the distance. It was not hard to see because very little else was around it.

We landed, and as we got off the plane, I said to one of the guides who met us, "Boy, is it ever hot here!"

It was 110 degrees or so.

He said, "This is the coolest day we've had in months."

Great.

Things changed dramatically in the next ten to fifteen minutes. A military-style jeep with soldiers in it raced up to the plane in a cloud of dust. The government had just been overthrown by militants. This would not be good for a group of Americans to land in Paraguay.

The pastors of the church where we stayed near Asunción made it quite clear to be careful and to let him do the talking. The soldiers looked pretty rough, and they shouted a lot. I understood a little of what they said. Not good.

We unloaded and headed to the living quarters near the church.

That night, we had a large gathering of the church community and workers from the community who were to work with us. We also met the orphans who lived at the church. We sang and listened to the pastors yelling praises.

I had never experienced anything like this in my life. I was blown away by the different feelings I had. I could not explain it. It was definitely a good thing though.

A young orphan boy from the church sat next to me. He was about eleven or twelve years old. This surprised me. Why did he want to be with me? As time went on, he was always with me. He went to nearly all the places we went unless the pastor told him he had to stay at the church.

The next morning, we started building a schoolhouse and a church building. We, Americans, should have taken notes because we could have multifunction buildings being used all year round like the ones we built. Just a thought. What a waste of resources and there is no comradery here in America.

The first day was unbearably hot. The native people had said siesta time was from eleven to two o'clock in the afternoon. We thought, *That's crazy. These people must be lazy and don't want to work hard.*

So we kept working. Big mistake. We got so tired due to the heat; some of us nearly passed out. I guess these guys were pretty smart after all. We had laid up the corners of the new church building using mud bricks made with straw and clay. The river people had made the bricks and laid them on the banks of the river to bake in the sun. The river people lived in cardboard houses, with only one room for the entire family. Their clothes were made up of one piece of cloth or leather hanging around their waist. The women had a small piece of material around their chest, not much in the way of attire.

The next morning, we were surprised to see all the bricks torn down and stacked in a pile in the middle of the area cleared for the building. The natives shook their heads back and forth. The interpreters told us they were saying they did not like the thing we were using. It was not good.

They had never seen a transit before, and they did not like it. What did they want us to use?

One of the natives said, "We will show you how to do it."

They brought a hose, filled it with water, and proceeded to use the water level to lay up the first several rows on the corners.

We let them finish and then checked it with the transit. Perfect. It took several days of us working with them to trust the transit or even to come close to it and then, finally, to look through it. They could not believe their eyes.

To see the native people using our modern equipment, the look of amazement on their faces, was something I would always remember.

That same look came over their faces at the church service that evening when the church told them about Jesus and how He would transform their lives through the cross. What a great feeling to see so many people's lives being changed in one moment at one place. You could feel the presence of the Holy Spirit in the building that evening. I had not seen or felt anything like this before.

We were stationed in Paraguay in the city of Asunción. Later, we stayed on the outskirts of the city for a week or so while we traveled and worked with the river people along the Amazon River.

One afternoon, three of us were taking the siesta time, which meant time off from our scheduled activities. We decided to walk through the small village and find some place to eat lunch. We came upon a small, one-room, little-mom-and-pop-store type of restaurant. You have never seen anything like it in our country. It was nothing more than a one-room shack.

We used our interpreter's guidebook and ordered a burger. It took us some time to try to explain what a burger was. We were in our glory after we ate and stood up from the small old and cracked wooden table that sat in front of the shack.

One of the local pastors who was working with our team walked up to us and asked, "What are you guys doing here?"

We explained how the burgers were good, and he said with a gruff tone in his voice, "Have you guys seen any cows since you have been here?"

We all said, "No."

He asked, "Where do you think they got the beef? Look around. What have you seen running around? What do you think you were eating? Dog. That's right, dog."

We all turned a different shade for a bit.

He added, "Remember when you guys got here, we said, 'Do not eat anywhere unless someone is with you from the church team here in Asunción?'"

The next day, we split the original fifty-person group into three groups. Our group got into a small, beat-up bus and headed to Brazil.

As we got into the jungle area, it was so thick you could see only short distances. Then we broke into a desertlike landscape. All of a sudden, a jeep full of guerillas armed with machine guns and ammo strapped everywhere rode up beside us. The oldest guy or kid was seventeen or eighteen years old.

We were all ordered off the bus at gunpoint, machine guns. The yelling back and forth from our guide and the lead kid was not something you wanted to experience. They searched the bus underneath, inside and out. They told us to turn around and put our hands on the bus. We thought we were toast. I know God heard a lot of prayers from of us that day. He should get a ton of prayers every day. They told us they were looking for guns and money. None of us had our original luggage or personal belongings. All we had was a small bag with a change or two of clothes, so they let us go.

We finished our work in Brazil, then headed back to the church where we started. I had forgotten to take the envelope with me on the trip to Brazil, so when we headed up a team to work in Argentina, I put the envelope in my bag. We got into the old bus again and started out.

We had stopped in a small city to get fuel and find a place to eat. We realized by this time that you did not want to venture off from the group.

But two of us decided to look around and check out the sites anyway. We walked down a small street and looked around at the buildings and the difference in the way people dressed from back home. Out of nowhere, we were shoved at gunpoint down to the end of the street to an abandoned building. We carried our personal bags with us. In those countries, possession was nine-tenths of the law. In other words, you own nothing other than what you have on you—nothing.

One guy grabbed our bags and dumped them out. He grabbed the envelope and held it up, and they yelled back and forth and ran off. Thank you, Jesus. They had what they wanted, it seemed. We double-timed back to the bus, climbed in, and sat down. The other guys were not back yet. We were not going to search for them at that point.

When they got back, we rode for quite a while.

Finally, we arrived at the church that needed help. We worked on several small outbuildings, trying to get them usable for the church as schools or shelters.

We put on roof supports and built a roof with some old tin sheets, branches, and long grass similar to straw.

The revival meetings at night were spiritually uplifting. The lead pastor spoke with authority and compassion all at once. I had never heard anything like it before. I was curious and uplifted at the same time.

Finally, we headed back to the church in Asunción where we started. Once again, when we went to the evening revivals or worked during the day, the young orphan boy went with me everywhere I went. I was so glad he was not with us when we were stopped by the soldiers. He was a great young man who needed someone in his life. I would not have wanted anything to happen to him. I will never forget the day we left. We all loaded up and went to the airport. He was there at the customs line trying to get to our plane. It was sad for me, but I also wish he could have come with us. He wanted so badly to go back to the United States with me.

I asked the pastor, "Please give him a ride back to the church and take care of him."

He assured me he would do so. I never figured out how he got to the airport.

Our flight back was a vastly different than the flight down. The plane was quite a bit newer, probably fifty years newer. We could actually talk to one another, and the seats had some padding on them. Thank you, Jesus.

I can look back and see now the blessing God bestowed on me big time.

I had been back home for several months when one morning, I woke up and remembered the dream I had the night before. I was to sell the factory. I thought, *Wow, what a dream!* It seemed so real. I did not give it a lot of thought and went on with my daily routine.

A couple days went by, and one of my friends came by and said, "My dad wants to buy your business."

I thought, *I didn't say anything to anyone or ever mentioned selling the factory.* Talk about spiritual forces.

He said, "I'll see you later."

About a week or so went by, and I was sitting in my office with the window facing the front parking lot wide open.

The door was wide open too because it was a hot July morning.

Vic—a big Italian guy, who I knew from my dad—drove in and yelled from his new, black Bronco. His son was the one who had said several weeks ago that "my dad wants to buy your business."

Vic shouted, "Come on! Get in. We're going for lunch."

I said, "I can't. I have some drawings to fill."

He yelled back, "Get in! We are going for lunch. I'm buying."

I didn't have a say in the matter.

"I'll be right out," I said, and off we went to the only little restaurant in town.

He ordered a bottle of wine, and we ordered food.

"Well, how much for your plant?" he asked.

I said, "I have no idea." I had no clue what to say. "I—I'll think about it," I said.

We talked for a while, and he took me back to the plant.

I thought, *I've had a lot of bad days in my life. I need a change. Only God could orchestrate something like this.* I was tired.

A week or so went by, and Vic pulled up to my window again, honked the horn, and yelled, "Get in! We're going to lunch."

"Okay!" I yelled, "I'll be right out."

We went to the same place to eat.

As we were eating, he said, "Well, how much?"

I had no clue what to say. I gave him a price, and he put out his hand and said, "You have a deal!"

We shook hands. That is how you seal deals. That is what my dad taught me.

I said, "I have only one condition: The people working for me stay."

He said, "Okay."

The next thing I knew, I was moving. It felt like I was dreaming. It all happened so fast and easily. So much was involved in the sale and transition, but it all went through without a hitch. Unbelievable. The light and the dark were once again very evident. Something or Someone was trying to get my attention spiritually. The light had definitely prevailed that day.

I had traveled a lot for business, and every time I went to this certain city on the east coast, I couldn't explain it, but I felt more at home than where I lived. I thought, *Why not move there to watch baseball and football games?*

When I was a little guy, my uncle had taken me to a Major League baseball game in that city. We sat behind home plate to watch the game. The memory was so vivid. The pitcher was Bob Veil, who threw pitches in the high ninety miles per hour. I enjoyed that day; it was one of my best days I remember as a kid. We drove around the city and ate lunch and then dinner after the game.

At the time, I thought, *This would be the coolest place to live!* Wow! What a time.

The Big Guy hears what you say from your heart. I now had an opportunity to live that dream from my childhood.

I only had an SUV and rented a trailer to haul my belongings. I did not have a lot of stuff. So I loaded up the truck and moved to Beverly Hills, that is…oops. Couldn't resist. I found a place to rent and a storage unit, and I settled in.

I found a church, which was not too far away. I could walk to it in about half an hour. The church was led by two pastors. One was full of life.

After I heard his message, I went to the altar. One of the elders laid hands on me, and she prayed for me. A warm feeling flowed through me.

It was the Holy Spirit. I had never seen or felt anything even close to that before.

The next couple days seemed as if someone had turned me into a new person, one who was at peace. Everything looked different to me in an amazingly good way. You might not believe me if I told you all the details. I saw everything through different lenses. Everything had a peace about it and amazement and joy. I could somehow sense people's spiritual lives. It is hard to put into words that makes sense unless you've experienced it yourself.

What a difference I felt. You might not believe this, but you need to hear it from the horse's mouth—yes, that end. Here it goes: I was lying in bed that night, sleeping. I was sound asleep or so I thought. Something picked me up out of my bed and threw me against the wall. I was about six feet off the floor, and I hit the wall above the top of a big, old double-paned window. I nearly went through that second-story window.

I hit the wall sideways and fell to the floor. I had major bruises on my side and head.

The really bad part though was I lost that good spiritual feeling I had experienced as a result of the prayer I received at the church. Sounds crazy, I know. But it's true. As I said earlier, other forces are at work every day, and most of us have no clue about them.

Something was not right about this place where I lived. It gave me the creeps. What it was, I was not sure. When I was there, I had a bad feeling inside, a feeling I never experienced before. What was it trying to tell me? Both before I had been slammed against the wall and especially after it, I knew I had to move and do it soon.

I got a newspaper and looked for work. I needed something to do. I saw a couple of ads and checked them out, and they were not what I had expected. For the moment, that was a dead end.

After a couple of months, I took a drive about as far away from civilization as you could get. I drove out of the city through the suburbs and into the countryside. I was almost in West Virginia. I parked my four-by-four, grabbed my fishing pole and vest, and walked about an hour to a small stream flowing through the hills.

I walked along a field with buffalo grazing.

One was on the edge of a large meadow, and when I came up over the crest of the hill, there stood a large buffalo. It was the largest animal I had ever seen that close in the wild. He snorted at me, and I thought, *If he charges me, I'm toast. This is not going to be good.*

I walked backward slowly and slid around the back of a large hemlock tree. Then I made tracks out of there as fast and quietly as I could.

That was not what I expected to do that day. I carried a fishing pole and my vest with all my tackle. Even if I had been hunting that day and carrying my gun, I still do not think I would have wanted to be that close to a buffalo. Maybe if I had Manny's elephant gun, I would have stood a chance.

I made my way down to the bottom of the valley to the stream and found a good spot to fish. I wanted to see whether there were any native brook trout. I caught a couple nice trout and was walking farther downstream. I found another nice curve in the stream where the water made its way under the bank. The trout like to lie in places like that because it's cooler on hot summer days. I remembered that the Indians I played with when I was younger had shown me many tricks to survive in the wild.

Knowing where to locate fish in a stream was one of them.

To my complete surprise, two guys came walking out of the bushes on the other side of the stream. One yelled, "Having any luck?"

I did not answer at first because I didn't think there was anyone within fifty miles of me. Finally, I said, "I got a couple nice 'brookies' here."

The other gentlemen, who had curly hair, said, "Come on upstream if you get a chance. We have a fire going upstream. We have good food and hot coffee. Come on down when you're done fishing."

I thought, *Why not?* I yelled back, "See you guys in a bit."

Think about that. Out in the middle of nowhere, I received a dinner invitation. What are the chances? I walked a bit farther upstream and met up with the guys.

We sat around the fire for a couple of hours telling fishing stories about the big ones that got away and reminiscing about past adventures. Again, Someone was watching over me. How else do you explain my meeting a couple guys in the middle of nowhere while I was in the woods fishing who would change my life in good ways I could never imagine?

The Big Guy sure has a sense of humor sometimes. He really must love us. For all the crap I had done in my life, He was still right there with me.

The two guys belonged to a local sportsmen's club. They told me they met every other Tuesday night in the summer at their clubhouse. They invited me to their next meeting. I thought, *Why not? My schedule is wide open.* I thanked them for the grub and said, "I'll see you guys in a couple weeks."

A couple of weeks went by, and I drove about forty-five minutes to the clubhouse. Right there at the club, they were having a catfish fishing tournament. I watched the guys pull out some pretty nice-sized fish. I thought, *Wow! I could fish here every night.*

I sat in on the meeting, and the guys I had met sponsored me. No one could join the club unless someone took responsibility for you for one year as a new member. They said they would cosponsor me as a new member.

I ended up being part of that club for twenty good and adventurous years for me and my family.

Chuck was a member of the club, and after a while, he said, "Hey, you mentioned you have a lot of stuff in storage. Why don't you keep it in my barn? It's dry, and it won't cost you a cent."

These guys were the kind of friends who were 100 percent legit.

Steve was another club member. He said to me, "Hey, my older brother, Tim, is rebuilding a house up the valley. We need some help. Come on up when you get a chance."

I said, "No problem. I'll see what I can do."

I gathered up some of my tools, put them in toolboxes, and then loaded them in my SUV the next day and headed to the small valley upstream from the sportsman's club to Tim's house. It was not hard to find. There was not a single other house around.

I drove up the old dirt road, unloaded my tools, and got to work helping remodel that old place. Tim was a young guy, just ready to get married. I thought, *A young guy getting married and having a place of his own to start out life together with his wife. How great is that?*

I helped for several weeks with framing, flooring, and any other work the house needed to have done.

One day, as I was working at the house, a new Buick pulled up, and a guy got out. He was dressed for office type of work: white shirt, tie, dress shoes, and dress pants. He had probably left his coat in the car. He started helping us for a while. Then he introduced himself, "I'm Tim's uncle."

We decided it was time for lunch. All of us had packed lunches, so we sat down to eat.

The uncle's name was Mark. He said, "This is my cousin's house. I appreciate you helping him. You're not taking any pay for helping?"

I said, "That's okay."

He asked, "Where are you working?"

I said, "Nowhere. I'm still looking. I'm good."

He handed me a card and said, "Give me a call when you want a job."

I said, "Thanks," and went back to work on the house.

One of the other guys, who was helping out, said, "There's going to be a wedding soon, so we better get finished with this house."

About a week or so later, I called the number on Mark's business card to make an appointment. Mark called me back the next day and told me to come in that day. Someone *is* watching over us. God knows our hearts, and when He sees one of his children looking for help, He is there to help us. We do not always see, hear, or listen to the direction God is seeking to lead us. He waits for us to make the right choices.

I met with Mark that day and filled out a long application that asked about skills and experiences. I also gave him my résumé. I thought, *Well, so much for that. I could use a good job, but how could they use me here?*

The next day, Mark called and said, "Can you come to a meeting tonight at seven o'clock? Don't be late and dress appropriately—coat and tie."

I said, "Yes, sir. I'll be there. Thank you."

That night, I drove to the other side of the city, to the office building Mark had given me the address; there was no GPS back then. I found my way to the meeting room. Many people filled the room. They sat facing a panel of dignitaries. I sat with Mark, and we listened as they discussed different projects for the next fiscal year. The dignitaries explained all the large construction projects going on in the city. As Mark and I sat there and listened to the speakers, Mark listened and never said a word.

I had no idea what I was doing there or why Mark had me come to a meeting where I knew no one except him. At one point during the meeting, the director of the meeting asked, "What about the high-rise project?"

Mark said, "We have that covered. I have the person in charge with me."

He told me to stand up and introduce myself to everyone. Talk about a gift from God. I was surprised. God had plans for me. The project had many issues, and I did not know about any of them.

After all, I had not even known about the project until a moment before. I had no clue what was in store for me, but it was okay. It turned out, I was to head up a five-million-dollar reconstruction of a major high-rise located in the east side of the city. I was told I would start the following Monday.

I had looked for a church when I moved to town but had not made it a priority. That Sunday morning, I attended a denominational church on the edge of the city. A young pastor spoke, and an elderly woman, who was part of the clergy and who wore a white-and-purple robe, stood in front when people went to the altar for prayer. I thought, *Great! This is a good time to give thanks for the job I just received.* I knelt and prayed. The lady put her hand on my head, as had been done in the other church. I had that same warm feeling flow through me again. What was it? Someone was definitely watching over me. I had no clue what the churches were doing in this area, but there was a spiritual difference.

The church I attended while growing up was all religion. We went through the motions, sang some hims (hymns) and hers. We gave our offerings into the plate so everyone could see we were good people. Then we went home and repeated the cycle just about every week. Sorry to get sidetracked here, but it's important to note.

8

Building a Better Tomorrow or What?

This first week on the new job was fast-paced. The first day, I was assigned two offices—one downtown and one on the east side of the city in the proximity of the worksite. All the bosses for city projects were located in the eastern city office complex. I was given an itinerary, which included a schedule of construction, due dates, material list, and a total cost expenditure for the project. This was in the area of total expenditures of around four to five million with some overrides.

The next day, I attended meetings all day. On Wednesday morning, I drove to my office on the east side. When I entered the building, I had to introduce myself to security and make my rounds to introduce myself to the various staff of each department. When I went into my office, I emptied my briefcase and went to work. I had much to do, a great deal of planning to ensure the project ran smoothly.

The next morning, I got to work before anyone but the night shift security.

As I worked in my office, I was quite surprised when one of the office staff came and told me she was my secretary. I had no idea one would be assigned to me so fast. She came in closed the door, sat on my desk, and asked, "Is there anything I can do for you?"

I said, "Yes, there is. Please get off my desk, and when you come in here, don't close the door, and we'll get along just fine."

Some people had other agendas than work. I was at the start of what was going to be a good experience and a nightmare all rolled into one. The forces at work were most definitely on the dark side. It does not matter what you do; you can't control others.

A few days later, I was told to attend a special meeting held downtown at a banquet-style event. The mayor was the guest speaker. His agenda was to review top projects for the city. Revitalizing the city was big on the mayor's political agenda.

I was not completely prepared when I was called on to address the specifics of our project, which was located in a low-income, high-crime area. I gave a short summary of my experience and a brief description of the timeline for our project. I gave my assurance that the project would be a success for the community.

Everything moved quickly.

The blueprints for the new building and the teardown of the existing building along with updates were forwarded to my office to overlay with the remodeling specifications and changes to be made after demolition was complete. I was to sign off all the materials for the building, which was a rebuild of fifteen floors. All had to be upgraded to be handicap accessible. I was also responsible for the removal of all demolition material.

I was not aware tenants still lived in the building on the first floor at the time. They would be shuffled from their existing rooms to the ground floors as we progressed with tearing off the top floors. Whoever thought that was a good idea was not very bright. It was also very unsafe in every manner.

This was hard on the tenants and proved to be difficult for the construction crews. I was amazed to see how money was used and abused to get the project completed. I'm sad to say it was all taxpayers' money.

Every day, people make choices. We choose to be believers or nonbelievers. God looks at a person's heart; money should not be your priority.

My personal life was boring at the time. I buried myself in my work again, but God had different plans for me. You will see what I mean as we continue. Again I was clueless.

I set up a worksite office where the lead foremen from each of the different trades set up shop. The plumbers, electricians, and carpenters were all involved. I went over everything we needed to accomplish with the foremen before the crews arrived to start working. We became a close group of men. I can look back now and see the differences between hard workers, in general, and hard workers with political agendas.

Somewhere along the line, the politician's decided to make the project a joint venture, with the construction project being one component and the site becoming a place for on-the-job training for vocational students. This was one of the few agendas that I agreed with from the start.

The idea was good, but I had no advance warning of the change. It became a full-time job in itself.

To handpick thirty students from a local high school, then set up the schedule for their training and keep my crews busy. It turned out to be the most rewarding part of my work and my life. I had no clue what would happen.

The students got a new chance in their lives because the school they attended wasn't known for a high graduation rate. Thank God, He had a plan in all the madness.

He did that through dedicated days of working and training. This was where I met my wife to be, who was also a workaholic. We helped each other, as she worked for a different organization that was working with this project, which included training the students in a classroom environment in addition to their on-the-job training. She was the director of the education department at the main office downtown.

The students enjoyed the classroom side of this project, and so did I. The basic skills they learned in math and other classes helped them with their work on the construction side of their work. All the students who completed this project and classes were guaranteed a good job with one of the union trades after completing the training allotted time on the project.

I could write an entire book about this project alone—maybe someday. I spent several days going over the prints for the existing building and the material list for the new construction project. As I did so, I was informed that the special construction elevator on the outside of the building was to be completed on Monday. It had to be built to carry away the asbestos-containing material that had been found in the building.

The main power supply we had in the basement was not sufficient to supply extra power for the 440 volt, three-phase power needed to power the lift for the elevator. We had to connect to the main power panel because the sub-panel was not sufficient.

I tried several times to gain access to the main power supply room in the basement, but security would not open the door for some odd reason. This was the first of many surprising and disastrous outcomes on this job.

I decided to stay late the next night. I bought a dozen donuts and a coffee and sat and ate with the night security guard. I asked him if I could go into the main panel room in the basement to check something for the elevator.

He said, "Sure, no problem."

He threw me the keys, and I opened the door to the main panel room hopefully to gain the power feed we needed.

When I went into the room, I could not believe what I saw. The prints clearly showed a complete upgrade of all the panels that had been done twelve years ago. It had been a million plus dollar project, which had been completed and inspected. A seal on the blueprints affirmed the inspection along with the necessary signatures.

What I found was the original main and subpanels from the nineteen fifties or sixties. No one had made a single change anywhere in this room for forty or fifty years or so. Talk about crazy. Where did all that money go and who signed off on the blueprints with certified seals of inspection? This was part of all the madness to come.

I decided to call my friend Mike, who was a manager of a large electrical supply distributor chain. I told him what I had and that I needed power from this panel. I needed breakers and materials fast because we were at an impasse.

Without power for the elevator, we could not bring down the asbestos material on the construction site. We were still on schedule, and I wanted to keep it that way.

Mike told me to pick him up early the next morning around six o'clock. I picked him up, and for two long days, we searched through Mike's different warehouses throughout the city until we found the parts we needed. The 440 volt, three-phase breakers to fit that ancient power supply were a difficult find.

Who would think when they got up for work one day that they'll be asking, "Hey, I think I'll need some electrical parts from the nineteen fifties or sixties?"

I turned my report into my boss.

The next morning, his secretary was at her desk at six-thirty in the morning. When I walked to my office, she came to me and said, "Mr. B. wants to see you."

I wondered, *What got them here so early this morning?*

My boss started asking how things were going.

I said, "Good, we're on schedule."

He held up my report on the electric panel problem and how it was solved and how that kept us on schedule. He started yelling and then shredded the report. He told me to forget all about what I had written on my report.

It never happened. Then he shouted, "Now get back to work."

I tried to no avail to ask, "What about the inspection and prints?"

Talk about crazy—more than a million dollars in upgrades to the electrical grid, the work "inspected" and signed-off, and the inspection seal attached. This was not a movie or fairy tale.

This was just the first of events I had to work through on this project. As my Dad would say, "Thugs wearing suits."

At the time, I did not give it a lot of thought either way. I was incredibly busy, and I tried my best to stay focused on the job at hand. I always spent a lot of time with my employees and worked with them as much as possible. That way, I could see firsthand how things were going and appreciate the hard work the crews did.

As construction continued, I noticed while going over inventory that some things were not adding up—literally. I made a report of what was needed for electrical fixtures for each room and totaled all other electrical materials needed to install in the entire building. Something was wrong. More than a 145,000 dollars had been overcharged, and we were way short on electrical materials needed to complete the project.

I checked and rechecked the purchase orders I had signed to the packing slips and went to the warehouse and inventoried all the electrical supplies we received.

I made some calls and then drove downtown to the storeroom main office where the electrical supplies had been ordered. This was not the same electrical company where my friend Mike worked.

I asked for the owner and waited a while.

When the owner came out and I introduced myself, he was very upbeat. I told him about my dilemma of the overcharge amount of, well, over a 145,000 dollars.

I said, "There must be some mistake."

His face got red, and he asked, "Who told you to come in here? Get out of my store!"

I was surprised, to say the least.

The next morning at six-thirty, which was when I usually arrived at work, even though I was not scheduled to start until eight o'clock, there was my boss's secretary again.

She said, "The boss would like to see you."

I went in and sat down.

This time, he started yelling immediately, "What are you doing?"

I explained how what we had paid for and what I had signed for were not the same numbers.

He yelled again, "Do not ever go into that store again."

Once again, he shredded my report. Talk about the good, the bad, and the ugly. This was definitely a bad and ugly side.

The good guys got runoff. They say money is the root of all evil. That is not correct: The love of money is the root of all evil. Our God is a jealous God. He wants the love of our hearts, and most people do not quite understand that. For an individual to understand there is an authority in this world over all our souls and spirits, we must know an owner's guide or manual has been issued. We can follow and use it for reference. I should have put my report in a Bible so my boss could have read it and perhaps had a change of heart. I wish it were that easy in the business world—or anywhere else.

With events such as these taking place, I do not know how, but we made it to the middle of the project, and we were still on schedule. Then I noticed our inventory for commercial-grade metal door jams was short from the number listed on the original order. No one stocked that size of commercial jams locally. They were special sized to meet the building specs. I checked everywhere, but I had no luck. We were looking at two to four weeks minimum for delivery. Not good at all. That would put a halt to the process we had set up for the crews.

That afternoon, I was eating lunch with a group of employees in the loading area. They were taking side bets on the coming Sunday's football game between the Steelers and the Browns.

I explained my predicament about the shortage of door jams just as lunch ended. As I walked down the hall, Mrs. Been, who had worked there for more than thirty years, said, "I overheard what you were saying, and maybe I can help."

She told me there was a warehouse owned by the city down by the river on the west side. Maybe I could check there to see whether they had the kind of metal door jams we needed. This was great news.

I told Mrs. Been, "Thanks, that's nice of you to tell me."

She smiled, flashed a broad grin, and said, "You're welcome," as she went back to her office.

I got in my SUV and drove to the address she gave me.

When I got there, it was a small brick building sitting at the back of an old asphalt parking lot. The building was red brick with old style steel windows. It did not seem big enough to store much of anything. *Surely, this is not a warehouse*, I thought. I was in for a surprise once again. Once again, what you see and what you get are two different things.

I walked in through the front door, which was wide open. Papers of all types were stacked to the ceiling everywhere. Only narrow aisles remained for walking. The entire building was only the size of a one-story house.

I walked around saying, "Anyone here?"

No one answered.

I walked up to a desk stacked with old papers and books, and there sat an elderly man with thick curly hair, even thicker wire-rimmed glasses, and a beard. He was kind of coarse-looking.

He was leaning back in his chair, facing the wall, and reading the local newspaper. He asked "What do you need?" not turning from reading his newspaper or moving at all for that matter. It was a "what do you want, and don't bother me" attitude. Remember, this was a city-owned building, and he was an employee on the city's payroll, believe it or not.

I told him my dilemma and what I needed for our project. He showed no concern or interest, but he pointed and said, "Over there. Take the stairs."

I said, "Thanks," and was on my way. I followed the stairs down, down, down. They contained a hundred steps at least.

When I got to the bottom of the pitlike stairwell, the door was locked. I looked up and thought, *There's no way I'm going back up those stairs to ask that guy anything.*

I could hear some faint noise on the other side of the door, so I pounded on it. No one opened it. I pounded a couple more times on this old double steel door, and finally, someone opened it. Standing there was a Chinese man, who said something to me in Chinese.

He pointed to his left. I could see the river just outside the building, and they were unloading fish packed in ice from a boat that was docked next to the loading dock. All you could smell was a pungent fish odor. I walked over to another Chinese man and asked, "Where is the warehouse?"

I do not think he understood English, but he pointed to the other side of the large room where they stored the fish containers.

I walked around trying to find an unlocked door. Finally, I found one, opened it, and could see nothing. The room was dark. I had to find a light switch. When I did, I turned on the lights, and I could not believe my eyes. It was a large room, bigger than a football field.

Materials were stacked everywhere. It was mostly new construction materials, but it also contained some used materials in excellent condition. Anything you could imagine were stacked everywhere: new windows of all sizes, all types of doors, building materials, and rows of appliances.

The building was packed in rows as far as I could see. I was looking at millions of dollars' worth of materials.

I got out my notepad and wrote down everything I needed for the door jams. It was all here, along with hundreds of other items we could use. This was great! We would be back on schedule on Monday. I looked around and thought, *How do I get out of here?* I made my way to a door on the one end wall with an Exit sign above it, turned out the lights, closed the door, and went outside.

I was next to a very large hill. All I could see was what looked like a thousand steps going up a steep hillside from the backside of the building. This was not the way I came in, but I knew by the terrain that the roadway where I drove in was somewhere at the top of that hill. I climbed the steps, and as I got to the top, I rounded the corner of the building, and someone grabbed me around the neck and tried to pull me against the building.

We got into a wrestling match. I flipped him over me and got him down and locked his arm and neck.

He said, "FBI."

I said, "Right."

I could see he had a gun. I was not letting go.

He said, "My badge is in next to my side pocket."

I looked over my arm and could see part of it. I proceeded to let him up.

He said, "You're under arrest for trespassing."

I showed him my ID badge and said, "I work with the city and the union. This is a city building."

He said, "We have had this building under surveillance for some time now. What are you doing here?"

This was all too crazy.

I said, "I'm out of here," brushed myself off, and got in my SUV.

By that time, it was late. I went home. My wife and I talked about the incident. We had been married recently. This job was getting to be dangerous, to say the least.

The next Monday morning, you know the drill: My boss who had eyes everywhere was in my office.

He said, "What in the world were you doing down there?"

I told him what we needed and what I had found.

He asked, "What am I going to do with you? You are causing me a lot of trouble."

Then he said, "Why don't you come work for me? I was subcontracted to finish this particular project."

He went on to offer me twice what I was making, all benefits, and many other perks.

He said, "I could use a guy like you. You know more of the people and what is going on than I do."

I said, "I would like to think on it. I'll let you know."

A lot of people who worked in this organization were under his direct supervision.

He said, "I'll make you vice president under me, and you will only take orders from me."

A few guys would literally have killed to get that job, and that was what was not so good. They were all wanting power positions.

The willingness to kill part was scary to me.

In the days ahead, I saw people on the job every day, who I had not seen before. I stayed focused on my assignments.

Have you ever had a feeling deep in your gut that something was not right? I felt that in those times; God is telling us through our inner selves, which is our spirits and the Holy Spirit all at once. Which way we turn is up to each of us. You and I have choices to make.

God always gives us an escape clause, not the clause like on the *Santa Clause* movie.

"You have to be wed in holy matrimony. Not valid in the state of Utah." No, not that type of clause.

This is a guaranteed clause. God knows our hearts and what we can and cannot handle.

I noticed for the next couple weeks that I was being tailed every day. Two guys in suits went everywhere I went. It was frustrating. They looked kind of like the two guys in the movie *Men in Black*.

I met with my boss, and I told him I would not be taking the position he had offered me as vice president. That was not good for me. I should have stalled a lot longer on the decision, but that was okay.

My job got very difficult for many reasons. I was now on his "ten most wanted" list.

I learned very fast that these guys were friendly as long as you were loyal to them and belonged to their organization. This was definitely a scene from an Al Pacino movie.

Several days went by, and I thought everything was business as usual. I was in my office on the construction site when two guys dressed as authority police officers told me at gunpoint that I had to leave the office on the construction site. I was the only one there at the time.

They said, "Leave everything. Don't touch anything, not your briefcase, notes, files—nothing."

I had tons of materials and personal items. These guys were good. They knew just where to wait for me and when was the exact time. I was toast or I would have been if the Big Guy was not looking after me as always. My guardian angel was there with me twenty-four seven.

I had parked my SUV beside the building on its west side. The two cops, who looked like thugs, took me down the back stairs, and one of them got a call on his radio.

He said, "I'll catch up."

Thank God for that.

We stepped outside, and some construction guys I recognized were walking across the lot.

I yelled quickly, "Hey, guys, come here a minute."

As they walked over, the cop faded back, and I kept the guys talking a bit. Then I walked casually to my SUV, keeping the guys with me in conversation as we walked. The cop stood next to the side door. I got in my SUV and drove away as fast as possible.

The next day, I resigned from the job. I had no choice in the matter.

I sent a long letter to the state attorney general's office explaining all that had gone on, noting I was not involved in taking any supplies or in any of the schemes for materials or for purchase orders I had signed when the materials did not match inventory. I explained in as much detail as I could remember. I lost many personal items, a computer, and all my logbooks and notes that day, but I got out alive. I had put my heart into that job and into the students at the site. What a change of events in my life. I was just glad to be alive and hopefully not pursued by any individual characters.

We experience many opportunities in life, some good, some not so good. If I had said "yes" to my boss, I could have been making tons of money to support my family, and my worries would have been over—nope! That was not the path I chose, and my gut feeling, my spirit, affirmed that choice.

All through my life, I have seen how evil can destroy my life and the people around me. Forces are at work in the spirit world all around us every day. We cannot see them, but I guarantee you that they are there. They can control or defeat us if we let them.

Each of us must make choices about which path we want to choose. I have seen rich men, poor men, weak men, and the strongest men destroy their lives by being misled into the darkest and saddest situations imaginable. Most were not aware of it until it was too late. Just like a demon would tell me on a vacation to come, "I know your steps before you take them," those paths are loaded with people whom Satan leads into your path to tempt you to stray his way. Choices.

During this time in my life, my wife, our boys, and I had joined a large church that had great pastors on staff. The place was growing about as fast as you could expect, and that was a good thing. People were getting saved, and you could see the changes in people's lives each month and how they grew more and more in their spiritual walks.

Again, I have seen the effects of how we can be divided both in the secular world and in the church when we let our emotions or feelings control us.

I still believe that the greatest of all enemies to the Christian faith is Christians themselves because we do not expect to be attacked from within.

If your past or present is not perfect, that is okay. God asks you to "repent." What a key word. We must ask for forgiveness when we pray to him and move forward in our lives. For example, when we are driving, our visibility is the entire windshield, and the small rearview mirror is for where we have been. This proportion is the same in life.

When people rely on their own personalities and not on God's Holy Spirit, their strengths and, even more, their weaknesses are magnified.

Satan will magnify your weaknesses, and you will be misled often. This is reflected in the book of Job. Job let fear into his life, and that opened the door for Satan to attack him. The saying goes like this: "Church would be a lot easier if it were not for all the people." Imagine that.

I look back and see the witchcraft and sorcery that has destroyed so many lives. I see the alcohol and drugs my friends took and, in my own life, drinking the hard stuff created so many problems. Speaking about this through real-life situations is so helpful.

If you were to talk to a detective, he would tell you, "Follow the money trail." Nine out of ten times, it will eventually lead you to the source of the problem. In the church, the pastor will tell you, "Follow the sin trail, it will lead you to the problem every time."

Have you ever seen a good movie and suddenly there is a turning point? You can see the change come over the actors or the music changes, and you know something important is coming. Well, imagine that right about now.

It was July, and my wife and I had made the decision to get baptized. We were to receive the Holy Spirit. If you ever want a life changer, I recommend you go through the necessary steps. After we had accepted Jesus as our Lord and Savior, we decided to move forward with the ceremony of water baptism.

All the gifts God had given me, which Satan had taken away, seemed to have been restored by God. The correct word here is "redeemed." This is like you are wired to run on 110 volts, and when you get baptized, you are now charged and running on 220 volts. What a difference. The magnification of the power of your spirit reaches others who are searching for help in God's eyes and are led to you not just by coincidence. That is how it works in the Holy Spirit world.

A lot of good churches are out there and a lot of good people too.

Holy Spirit–filled churches follow the whole Bible, not just certain books. You must make choices and learn how to discern right from wrong. Being filled with the Holy Spirit and having Jesus as your Savior will guide you with your decisions. This is the best and only way you can stay on track and feel God's love and spread God's love everywhere you go. Life is a journey, and it is best to follow His guide while we are on it.

One thing for sure is pick up the Bible if you are a believer or even if you are not and you want to make a decision about your next move. You have an entire lifetime to decide what to do. I suggest you start by reading the book of Acts three times. Yes, that is correct—three times. The first time through, say a prayer each time you read a segment or chapter. Once you have read the book, say a prayer for the Holy Spirit to give you guidance about what you have read. Think about it for a couple days or even a week, then read it through a second time. Each time you read anything in the Bible, which is God's word, it will work on your heart and spirit, showing you and giving insight to what you have read.

The third time through Acts, keep an open mind to what you are reading and be attentive.

You will be amazed at the information you'll receive and how the book of Acts will help you when you are looking for a church or pastor who will be Holy Spirit–filled.

Dos and Don'ts

As the years went by, I made a transition to a totally different line of work. Our family through the years were still attending the same church, and you could see major changes going on in this large church and sadly not for the better. Pastors were let go because of misrepresentations and the power of greed started taking over.

People who were employed by the church were not paid for their full hours; information was posted on computers to trap people and release them when the church had other plans for the staff and on and on. If you had a lot of money to donate, the power was definitely turned up for you and your siblings.

You could feel the presence of the Holy Spirit in the church. Then it was gone. It was like sitting in a Walmart department store or a warehouse at a business meeting. It was spiritually empty. Again, Satan will always try to steal, kill, and destroy what we have built up, and if you are sinning, you are opening the door for him to come in. Many of the families who had been foundational were going elsewhere.

The road back is very simple: Repent honestly with a decisive heart. Then get back on track and ask for forgiveness from the Holy Spirit.

Meanwhile, back at the ranch, we were meeting a lot of new people and interacting with friends and doing activities with our family. This opened a whole new arena of associates for us. Our kids were growing up. We were making a lot of changes in our schedules. One of those new people was a local homeopathic doctor whose family we knew from different activities we participated together in the community. We had learned a lot regarding health issues from him, especially that what you put in your mouth relates to your overall well-being and staying healthy.

The journey of most successful people starts with having a goal and trying to achieve it. Having determination, skills, and positive attitude determine your outcome. Being Spirit-filled helps the most, that is, Holy Spirit–filled.

For example, doctors see their patients being healed.

The advice concerning the foods they eat and how God has made our bodies to heal themselves, they are amazing. Dr. Rompa found this quite rewarding; he would always tell his patients to pray over their supplements before taking them.

My wife and I and our families were grateful for what we learned and how our health improved.

One afternoon, the doctor and I were eating lunch together at a plaza close to his office. We finished eating, and when I took him back to his office, caution tape circled his parking lot, and several unmarked police cars sat in the lot. The local district attorney's office was shutting down his business, and he was not permitted in the building to get anything out. Does that sound familiar? The dark side was making its presence again.

A couple days went by, and we talked often about what had happened. He and his wife had adopted their friends' kids after their parents died in an accident. The problem was the children's grandmother, who just happened to work at the district attorney's office, wanted custody of the children, and she was not happy. She did everything she could to ruin his business and get the kids. She had stated the money they received from the estate from the kids' parents was to be used only for the kids.

The doctor and his family had to move when they adopted the kids, and they also bought a bigger vehicle so they could transport all their children. This did not meet the grandmother's approval. So she pushed until she got her way. The court ordered them to sell their house and car and put the money back into the estate fund. Satan's work and workers come in all sizes and shapes. Sometimes they even look pretty and smile.

The doctor and his family were humiliated. He lost his business but not the kids. He was heartbroken, but his family was still together. The forces, sometimes you can see and hear them; and this time, evil showed itself in visible ways.

He and his family moved away and started over in another state. He is now very successful even more so than he was when he lived here. We sure do miss having him here as a close friend, and his patients were all dispersed. Many of them had been with him for a lot of years. Fortunately, he did not give up, and his business was restored. This is what it means to experience being redeemed. His business is better than ever, and his family is happy.

They are blessed and highly favored. People have no idea about the darkness that is out there. Remember, though, the light always prevails. As John Wayne said, "Right will prevail. Right will prevail."

John Wayne also said, "It does not matter where you go, God has already been there." So true.

As time went by, our boys and I developed a routine at night. I told them stories. Sometimes they came from the Bible or other books. Then I said a prayer over each of the boys out loud before they turned in for the night.

One night, as I finished praying over our youngest son, I said, "I pray someday God will use you as a pastor or minister in some way."

As I was walking out the doorway, my youngest son said, "Dad, why don't you become a pastor someday?"

I paused and said, "That sounds good. Love you guys. Pleasant dreams," and I turned in for the night.

The next day and for weeks to come, I could not get what my son had said out of my mind. I prayed about it, and my wife prayed about it. We talked and both agreed; my thoughts, my prayers, and the dreams I had had for a long time agreed with God's words spoken through our son.

I contacted some friends who had gone through the process of becoming a minister. It took a lot of schooling and training and prayers, but it was worth it. At times, it was hard on our finances. Again, the Big Guy, God, knew what was in my heart all along.

I could see clearly Satan did not want me to go down this road earlier in my life. I believe the more potential you have to spread God's word spiritually and physically, the more Satan will do everything he can to mislead you and bring the wrong people into your life. You make the choices, some good, some not so good.

I did finish my schooling and got ordained as a father and a husband, and I have continued classes to expand my knowledge and degree over the years.

I thought I had given God my all, but He knows your heart's desire. Boy, was I wrong. I was responsible for our finances. I thought after we saved so much money, we would be secure, and I would be happy or content.

Again, God knew my heart, and my attention was not on Him. I invested some of our money through a friend of ours. One day, a major change rocked the stock market, and I lost all our savings. This devastated us. All our savings were gone. I took it extremely hard. I was devastated. God had my attention. It took a while to sink in, but I realized my love of money and my relying on myself for security for myself and my family were wrong. The only security for my family and me was God.

We had been baptized in the Holy Spirit, as my wife and I and our children all received the baptism. As they made the decision on their own and they understood Jesus was their Lord and Savior, they were cleansed by Jesus and given the power of the Holy Spirit. The reasoning for bringing this into the equation is that we were all equally yoked. They spoke in tongues and had a direct line of communication with Jesus. This was so different from my past. Back then, when I got into trouble, it usually got worse and never resulted in a good outcome.

This was different in a good way.

This was what we needed to come full circle when a family problem arose, such as this one, losing our finances.

We prayed every day for God's blessing, and I worked diligently to get our business back on its feet. How important it is to know God works in your life and, as important, how He brings people to you and works in their lives. Sometimes we have no clue when or what situation will come along, and it will happen.

As time passed, one day, an individual who owned a large company that we had done some work for in the past had a problem with a company he hired to do a project on one of their properties. The project was working on a large shopping plaza. The owner called me to look at the job site and to give my opinion on how to correct the problem. He was very irritated by the outcome and appearance of the work that had been done.

We drove to the site, a shopping plaza on the other side of the city.

After I did several days of research, I was asked how to solve the problem. I found a solution using the product that was approved by the owner of the plaza that would correct the problem. I was asked by the owner to do a sample area on one of his plazas in our area.

I rented some equipment and put a new design on the building and did the sample area as requested. I called the owner and requested an inspection meeting at the proposed site. The next morning at eight o'clock, the owner pulled up, got out, and inspected the work. He was quite surprised. He put out his hand and said, "You have all the jobs. Excellent work."

There was something different going on. I was at work, and I could feel the presence of the Holy Spirit there with me. I thought this only happened at church.

I just stood there astounded as he drove away. For several minutes, I stood on the edge of the curb as cars went by, my hand still out. All I could think was, All *the jobs. What does that mean?*

The next week, we received an email with all the projects to be completed for the upcoming year. We did receive all the contracts, and of course, we encountered some problems, but the cool part was: God redeemed us financially, plus we were blessed with the opportunity to save a lot of souls.

Just to show you the power of the Holy Spirit, when you charge your batteries by praying—and I mean praying—in tongues, remember when you read the book of Acts, what happened with the apostles?

Just a thought.

For example, I was working with our crew on the biggest project of all the shopping plazas. I was on my knees on the edge of a cement curb sidewalk at the end of the building. It was July, and about six-thirty in the morning.

I was working diligently when I looked up and a man about six foot four or five wearing shorts, a tank top, and a red bandana on his head was jogging around the corner. He ran up to me, stopped, and looked down at me.

He was in his sixties, I would guess. He started talking to me and telling me all about his life. He was a retired narcotics cop. He went on to tell me how his son had committed suicide in their bathroom. He could not break the door in when his son was overdosing in the bathroom, so he got a ladder, climbed up outside, broke the window, and climbed in.

"Sadly," he said, "it was too late. My son was dead." As he told me, tears flowed down his face. He said, "My wife blamed me. It was all my fault."

He went on to say his wife had also passed, and he was living alone. He said, "I have nothing to live for anymore."

I thought, *This guy is ready to check out.* I asked him his name. When he told me, I said, "Harry, do you have any family left?"

He said, "Yes, I have a daughter who lives in a neighboring town."

We talked briefly, and I asked, "Harry, are you a believer?"

He said, "I'm Catholic. I think so."

I said, "Harry, every morning when you get up, look in the mirror and say out loud 'Jesus loves Me' several times. Do the same before you go to bed every night. Say it out loud looking in the mirror. 'Jesus loves Me.' Two people hear this: you and Jesus."

All this took only about ten to fifteen minutes tops. All of a sudden, a couple other joggers, Harry's friends, came around the corner.

Harry snapped out of it quick and stood up straight, and they all took off.

Okay, I thought, *that was an experience I will never forget.*

God has plans for all of us, some quick, some slow. We never know.

Several weeks went by, and "Suzie went and left us for some foreign guy." Oops, sorry, couldn't resist. I was working in the same plaza. It was early morning again, and Harry ran up to me. It was not the same Harry I met before. He had a smile on his face, and his demeanor had changed. He stuck out his hand and said, "Thank you. I took your advice, and it worked."

He said, "I got ahold of my daughter who is a believer also, and I went to church with her and her family and got saved that morning. It was the first time I can remember being in church for quite some time."

We talked briefly, and off he ran to finish his morning jog.

Thank you, Jesus!

Satan, you can get lost.

That was God using people—this time, me—to speak to another person. Next time, it will be you.

A friend of mine named Heath, who was a new pastor too, had started a church on the border in another state. They were meeting in a middle school on Sundays for service.

One morning, I received a call from Heath. He was not doing so well. He was devastated.

He was not a full-time pastor supported by his church, at least not yet. He said, "I lost my job, and the church lost our lease to hold services in the school."

We talked for a while, and the Holy Spirit gave me wisdom.

I said, "Be here on Monday morning at six o'clock and don't be late."

I explained to him that he could work with us, and we would help him with the problems with the church location.

After some prayer, my wife and I agreed we could help the church. After some searching, a realtor who is now an active member of the church, found a building. The rent was way out of line, and they wanted the church to offer four times what a respectable bid would have been for the building.

The church had no money to cover this.

I said to the pastor, "Our tithes from the business would help."

Believe it or not, it was what the church needed to put a deposit on the building and cover their immediate costs.

Only God could orchestrate something like that at the exact time and amount needed.

They went from sixty to eighty people on the weekend when they moved into their new location to more than five hundred people attending on a given weekend now. Look at how many people have been blessed by a few faithful believers—and how many lives have been saved for eternity.

The saying goes: "This is the first day of the rest of your life." That day is when you are saved when you accept Jesus as your Lord and Savior. Your name is written in the book of life; in that moment, your eternal future is secure.

God uses people over and over again to reach people. Believe me, in our lives, we have experienced many obstacles in the way, and it was not all as easy as it sounds, but the outcome is there.

Many lives had been saved, marriages had been impacted, and people had been healed. Oh, by the way, all the money we lost several years ago, we worked hard, and all of it was restored. Thank you, God. The key word here is redeemed.

There is something important that needs to be said before we go any longer.

God is speaking to all of us. He wants to use all of us in our daily lives as believers. We only need to have faith and learn to listen. The good, bad, and ugly will always exist. By ugly, we mean disgusting way of living in God's eyes.

10

The Great Deceiver

God knows your heart and the hearts of other believers also. For example, one morning, I had been working on a project for school and was studying and doing some research. The Holy Spirit spoke to me and said, "Take a ride." It was not an actual voice but a knowing or inclination. Believe me, when it happens, you will know.

I asked my family, "Hey, do you guys want to ride along?"

They all said, "Sure, let's go."

I had been on a mission for some time now, working on compiling newspaper clippings, articles from the Internet, and notes from information on the radio over the years. I was very aggravated at what the ACLU was doing to take the Ten Commandments out of schools, stopping teachers from praying and taking nativity sets down at courthouses and other government properties. This was very upsetting to me. I had been praying for this to change over the years. I had even gone as far as making an appointment with one of the most powerful attorneys in our area. We spoke at length about the problem and how movie stars and politicians were giving millions to support such a group of atheist people and how disgusting it was to me. I got carried away again, but that was okay—real-life situations.

Where were we? Oh, yes, we all piled into our van: my wife, our boys, and I, and off we went for a ride. It was after Thanksgiving, and some people had decorated their homes for Christmas. We were driving around the community, and God spoke to my heart and said, "There's one." We drove a little longer, and again, I had that inclination in my spirit, "There's one."

We drove for a little while longer looking around and enjoying the ride. We got back home and ate lunch together, and I went back to work.

A couple weeks went by, and God spoke to my heart again and said, "How many were there?"

I had no clue what He meant.

Then He said, "How many of their houses were there?"

I thought, *I have no clue what You are talking about. I have no clue what* their houses *meant. Sorry, I am a little thickheaded, God, sometimes.*

I said, "Their houses."

God said, "Two post offices."

God spoke to my heart again and said, "How many were there?"

I had no clue what He meant.

Then He said, "How many of My houses were there?"

I said, "Your houses?"

It was embarrassing. I had no clue.

God said, "Seven."

"Okay."

God said, "My houses—churches."

I should have gotten that one.

"How many of my houses had nativity scenes?"

I said, "None."

"How many of their houses had Christmas decorations?"

I said, "I have no clue."

God said, "My houses are being forgotten. Satan is the great deceiver. You and millions of other people are spending their time and resources on the wrong buildings."

God's buildings, the churches, are being neglected: no nativity sets or decoration, plaques, or any type of landscaping and no improvements in front of the churches in our area.

God said, "I do not want you wasting any more of your time being deceived."

I would never have seen it that way in a million years. The Big Guy is patiently waiting for us to come on board. If you are listening, God is speaking to you more than you realize.

As time went by, our family's view of the world around us was changing. That was a good thing. It was a God thing for sure. One of the biggest influences in my journey was Pastor Greg, whose wife changed my wife's life forever.

My wife was raised a Methodist in the Midwest, and the church she attended was very traditional religion.

One evening, Pastor Greg's wife walked toward us down the large hallway after a church service. I could see the glow about her. She was full of the Holy Spirit. My wife was struggling with how she felt about being totally accepted by Jesus.

I could see the transformation as she explained to my wife Jesus loved her just the way she was.

She said, "You do not have to change a thing in your life."

Peace came over my wife, and she knew that she knew. When you are present in a situation like this, words cannot describe the transformation that takes place. It is life coming into a dead body. You are saying your wife was dead? She was before she was saved.

She was saved, but she did not fully believe.

That is what's vital. Her faith is what Jesus wants. That is what being born again means—totally accepting Jesus.

As time went by, I did not realize all the changes taking place in my life. Work was work. I still witnessed to people everywhere I went. I think I had led more people to Christ in stores, at job sites, and at gas stations than in all the churches we had worked in combined.

I sure wish pastors and churches would get out into the community and socialize with people in their areas on a regular basis. The local church has been the heartbeat of our society for many years.

That is the way it was before all our electronic devices and modern conveniences kept us secluded and away from one another to some extent. Remember: Divide and conquer is Satan's MO.

Several years ago, we were traveling to Florida to visit friends. I know I said this before, but I feel it is very important to show how we spend our time and energy to show our love to our families.

It seems when you plan to go anywhere as a parent, you must work double before and after you leave. I had put in long days before we left and was tired and ready for a vacation. This is to all the mom and dads out there: When you are on a limited budget and traveling, sometimes you have spent so much time getting everything ready that when the time comes to leave on vacation, you're exhausted.

We drove off early in the morning and were planning to camp on the way down to save money. We knew we would have some family fun in the process. We drove for about eight hours. It was late Saturday afternoon. We stopped for a break. There was an early evening service at a small church in the hills of a small coal mining town on our way. A young pastor was getting ready for the service. This was his first or second service as a new pastor.

I introduced myself. He had a lot of questions. He was not experienced at all in the ministry.

He was a young man with a wife and kids. He gave me a quick snapshot of his life as a husband and a believer. He was a coal miner and had been arrested and was about to lose his job and family. At that moment, he trusted Jesus, turned it all over to Him, got saved, and went through the process of reading the Bible daily and praying for wisdom. The church gave him an opportunity to step forward to lead the congregation.

The prior pastor had left without any notice, and the church needed a leader. Talk about stepping out in faith.

During the service, people were asked to come up front for prayer. The pastor's mother-in-law came forward. She asked for a prayer for an illness that was getting worse. She had been fighting this sickness for several months. I went forward and laid hands on her, and we prayed. I was tired and did not know what was about to happen. I should have known better and been spiritually stronger in a situation like this.

We ate dinner after worship with the pastor and an elder. They had invited our family to their treat at a small Mexican restaurant. We talked for some time, and our trip with many hours of driving on each leg of our journey was making for a long day. We told the pastor and the elder "thanks" for the meal and fellowship.

We got back into the truck and back on the road again. *Me and you and a dog named Boo travelin' and livin' off the land.* (Couldn't resist.) After three or four hours of driving, I was getting very tired. Several times, I felt myself getting very angry or upset over nothing special that was said in the truck as we were driving south to our next stopping point my wife had laid out for us.

I did not feel the same. I was easily irritated. Maybe I was just too tired. That was not the case at all.

That night, we found a camping ground, set up our tent, and built a fire. The kids roasted some marshmallows and made some smores, and we all got our sleeping bags in the tent and called it a day. I had not noticed we had set up the tent in the campsite under a very large cypress tree. After a short while, everyone went to sleep, nearly everyone, that is, except me. I was wide awake.

I was lying there, and I could smell something. I could hear something rustling near the tent. It was a good thing I didn't get up to check it out. I put my face up to the tent, and right outside was a whole clan of skunks. I woke my wife very quietly. We watched quietly through the tent so as not to cause any ruckus with the skunks. What a disaster that would have been if they had all sprayed our tent. We watched them for a while.

They were looking around the campsite for something to eat, and not finding anything, they moved on. Several hours went by, and I was very tired but still very much awake. The locusts in the tree above us were so loud it was a constant buzzing. For some reason, it seemed their buzzing, squelching sound was being magnified. They were so irritating I could not get to sleep.

I got up, opened the tent, and walked down the gravel road a little away and went into the cement block building that was for the campers who were registered at the park here in South Carolina. This was the side where everyone showered and cleaned up. It had two sides: a shower area and a restroom. A row of sinks lined the wall next to me. I realized how quiet it was. I could not hear the locusts outside. It was very hot, and the building had rows of large screened windows on the top of each wall for ventilation. I thought, *That's weird. I cannot hear the sound of the locusts anymore. Great! Maybe I can get some sleep.*

I walked back up the short gravel road to the tent, unzipped it, and zipped it up again to keep the skunks out and laid down. The locusts started up again. They were so loud; I couldn't sleep again. I thought, *I know what. I'll go into the truck.*

I got up, opened the tent, zipped it up, walked to the driver's door, and got in. It was very hot and humid.

I thought, *I'll start it up to turn on the air conditioning and go to sleep. Great!*

I put the key in, went to start it, and thought, *No way. Wait a minute, the truck is backed up to the tent. That would not be good at all. The fumes would suffocate everyone.*

I got out of the truck and went back into the tent.

It was way past midnight, and we were planning to leave early in the morning. Then I thought, *Hello! Why didn't I think of this earlier? I'll pray in tongues until I go to sleep.*

After praying for a while, I started choking really bad. I kept praying.

I felt something forcing me and choking me. I kept praying, and there was a "pop" feeling, and a black cloud-like image was before me.

It said in a deep gruff voice, "How old are you?" Before I could answer, it said, "I am over a million days old." Then there was a short pause, and it said, "I know your steps before you take them." Then it was gone.

I thought, *That was weird, way too weird.* I was so tired I closed my eyes and fell asleep immediately.

We all got up the next morning, and I explained what happened. To the best of our knowledge, the lady I had prayed for at church had that creepy demon in her, and it came out of her; and when I was so tired, I was not aware or strong enough to cast the demon away, so it lingered near me.

As we were preparing to pack up and start on the last leg of our trip, I was praying, and the Holy Spirit revealed to me what was said. The "over a million days" was easy to figure out. "Knowing my steps" was weird. The same number of demons are here on earth that were here from the beginning of the fallen angels. They do not multiply or grow.

That demon had been in thousands of people over the years, and the Holy Spirit showed me that the demon knows how people will react before they do because of the thousands of people it was in before. It can see the same patterns over and over again.

He said, "Now you know how people feel when you cast demons out of them."

I thought, *Thanks, you could have just told me. It would have been much easier.* If that had been the case though, I would not have understood as fully as I do because I experienced it. It was still very weird.

Just a thought: There is a heaven, and there is a hell, and everyone is going to one or the other. So many people I talk to say, "I'm a Catholic" or "I'm a Lutheran." I do not think when you get to heaven God is going to say, "All you Catholics over there, and all you Methodists over there." We are all from the same clan. This is to clarify that the spirit world knows no boundaries, especially not the artificial ones we create.

Back to our vacation, we finally got to Florida and met our friends. We had a good time together for the afternoon.

We always did because our families were very close. We had been friends for a long time now. We met one another while we were attending the big church where we got baptized.

That evening, we got a hotel room with a pool for the families to swim together in the mornings because the kids like to swim, and we do not have a pool at home.

The next morning, the boys wanted to swim before we left to meet our friends and have a fun day together.

I was sitting at a table, reading a book from one of my theology classes and watching the boys dunk each other.

A stocky guy with a thick beard walked by and said, "Hey, mate. You know, I am from England. That's why I have this crazy accent."

I stood up, and we introduced ourselves and shook hands.

He said, "I see you're reading a book about the Bible. My job back home is I work in a large warehouse, mate. We ship items all around the world." He went on to say, "My wife and I enjoy riding our Harleys. We wanted to see where they make the bikes here in the US and tour the factory."

He went on to say, "I brought a Bible with me. Imagine me of all people bringing a Bible with me on vacation. I just can't get it out of my mind. I don't understand."

I said, "I do. Do you want to know why?"

He looked at me for a second and said, "Yes, I sure do," with a puzzled, inquisitive look.

I told him the story from Adam and Eve to Jesus and how the keys were there for him to accept and have Jesus as His Lord and Savior. He would also have the same authority and power from the Holy Spirit as Jesus does today sitting at the right hand of God, the Father.

He asked, "What do I have to do?"

I said, "It is very easy. Do you repent of all your sins?"

He said, "Yes, I sure do, mate."

I said, "Do you believe Jesus is your Lord and Savior and He died on the cross to forgive your sins?"

He said, "Yes."

I said, "Do you accept Jesus as your Lord and Savior?"

He said, "Yes, I do, mate."

I said, "Welcome to the family of believers. You are now a new person in Christ. Your old self is gone. You were dead. Now you are alive. Please mark this day in your Bible."

He had tears running down his cheeks.

The first words out of his mouth were, "I'm going to, you know, mate, spread God's word everywhere I go."

Just then, his wife and daughter came around the corner of a long stone wall along the walkway next to the pool.

She said, "Honey, what did this man do to you?"

He still had tears flowing down his face.

He said, "Imagine me, of all people, accepting Jesus and carrying a Bible around."

His wife gave him a big hug.

He said, "Thanks, mate," and they all walked toward their room.

I felt it was only a matter of time before the whole family became believers and began spreading God's word everywhere they go.

God has plans for that man and his family the same way He does for you—that is right, you—the one reading this book. This book is blessed of the Holy Spirit, and now you are too. Even if that was the only reason, we went to Florida that year; it would be okay. We finished our vacation in Florida and headed home. God needs people, and we need God.

11

People Are Searching

That fall, sometime between Thanksgiving and Christmas, our family was shopping at Costco. It was Sunday morning after church, and they had taste-testing tables set up to sample food and display their items to taste. What a great concept. It would be kind of cool if churches could use this concept. Set up several booths and give a cookie or treat and a couple verses from the Bible for people to get a taste of it and how it can change their life. Sell them the Bible at a discount they can't refuse.

Where were we? Oh, ya, my son and I were pushing the cart, and the store was filled with people. It was time for holiday shopping, and food was on everyone's agenda. The rest of the family went one way to grab some fruit and veggies, and we turned the corner where the vita mix lady was up on a platform blending something good for samples. A group of maybe fifty people at the least watched and waited to try something. As we were near the back of the crowd, she said, "You, you look different." She wore a microphone on her cheek.

Then she pointed to my son also, "You look different too. You're happy."

I made my way up front.

She was still on the mic. She said, "Why are you so happy?"

I said, "Do you really want to know?"

She said, "Yes, I do."

I said, "I have Jesus in my heart."

She said, "I knew it."

She took off her mic and gave it to the other person working with her in the booth.

By this time, the rest of the family showed up.

She said to my wife, "God has been tugging at my heart, and I cannot get it out of my mind."

My wife talked with her for a while and recommended she find a good Spirit-filled church in the state where she lived so she could charge up her spirit.

You are like a battery, and praying, especially praying in tongues, charges your spiritual battery. This gives you the strength for people searching to seek you out and to find the Holy Spirit too. Cool, isn't it?

You see, if God can use someone like me, He can use anyone. Having Jesus in your heart, speaking out loud daily in prayer, and praying in tongues build up power and strength in you that God uses to help other people. Having faith and believing are all up to you. It is very private, just between you and God the Father who loves you uncondi-tionally. He will always be there for you now and through your life and through eternity.

Time went by, and our church planned a mission trip to Costa Rica. I had been on several trips before. I mentioned the one to Paraguay, Argentina, and Brazil. I had also been to Mexico. I was away from the government crap or so I thought. I did not want to go unless all our family went together. We had some major stumbling blocks come up, most of which were financial. The comingling of funds at the big church was very disappointing to us. People donated money to the church in our family's name to help us pay for part of our trip.

As time went by, we were short of the amount of money needed for the trip. One of the families who donated money asked if they should donate more money and how much we were short.

I said, "What? No one donated anything to our account."

Shortly after, other people came forward that they had donated money into our account.

After quite a bit of time in calls and contacting the right people, the individual who had changed the deposits was revealed. Not good in the church.

We put it behind us, and it nearly put the dampers to the trip for us. The god with the little g gets in some places sometimes, so you must be sure he is truly gone.

We overcame the hurdles, and off we went to Costa Rica as a family.

Just a thought: If Satan sees you are going to do great things for Jesus, he will do everything he can to derail you and your family.

The flight to Costa Rica was very long, and when we got there, the rooms where we were to stay were bogus. I meant they were in very bad shape, as in not livable at all.

The money the group paid for the rooms and food went somewhere, but it surely was not for the accommodations and the food. We expected. We ended up eating every day at the church, and the ladies at the church prepared the food for us each day. We had to find other accommodations fast. We were fortunate the church helped us get settled in rooms for all of us.

We spent a lot of time helping the church remodel to make classrooms for the school on the second floor. The building was a large retail store with space for storage for a warehouse used by local stores.

We did a lot of construction work on the building at the church. There were walls to build and prime and paint. The plan was to make a Christian school at the church for grade school classes for local kids. Our schedule was very tight. We had a lot to accomplish in little time. We only had ten days.

About the third day, one of the men with us came up to me and asked if he could sit down with me because he had a lot of questions about his beliefs. We sat and talked for about an hour and a half.

During our conversation, I discovered the reason he signed up for the trip was the girl he liked was on the trip too. He confessed he was an atheist. He had never heard the Gospel explained as I explained it before. He said, "Thanks," and went back to work.

The next morning, I had seven or eight men come to me who were all regular churchgoers; some of the guys were ushers, others were security or maintenance workers. They asked me, "Can you tell us the same information you told Tony yesterday?"

We talked for two hours. They asked a lot of biblical questions that were very basic.

I was surprised they did not know. It was all good.

They said, "Thanks," and were very appreciative to have the personal time to have answers and explanations for a lot of their spiritual and biblical questions.

We were thousands of miles from home, and to answer that many questions and take that amount of time to talk to believers who attended church pretty much every Sunday surprised me.

It goes to show that some people go through the motions and are caught up in the everyday hustle and bustle of life—even church life—delegating their time and too much time just volunteering. They do not take the time to learn the basic teachings and facts, in this case, of what the Bible says about their authority and what Jesus said about their lives. All these guys left different than they came.

The presence of the Holy Spirit was amazing to experience. I was blessed to have the opportunity to give a sermon at an old church in the city during the evening service, and the healings that took place were evidence the Holy Spirit was moving.

We had planned some outreach trips, but we could not accomplish them without the government's approval.

We were not in the USA, where we can come and go as we please without government approval.

Just a thought: When you cast your votes each year, your life matters.

The government approved our outreach to the local hospital. It was new and quite nice. It was a large building for the area, and people came from all over Costa Rica to be treated at this hospital. We packed into the bus and brought all our extra Bibles and skit materials.

We planned to put on Bible skits in the main lobby next to the hospital's main hallway. We presented the Gospel message outside in front of the hospital. There was a large sitting area in front of the hospital with benches. We were starting to get a crowd gathering around, watching us. Many kids and adults accepted Jesus as their Lord and Savior; this was so exciting to see how the people were like sponges.

We gave out Jesus bracelets and T-shirts to the kids. We gave Bibles and pamphlets to as many people who wanted them.

We had asked the hospital administrator if we could go into the rooms and pray with the patients, but we were denied access. God had different plans for us though. After we performed the skits and talked with the people for several hours, which the administrator had watched the entire time, we were told we were permitted to take four people to each floor, this included the interpreters, to pray with the patients. We did not even have to ask.

We were permitted to take our interpreters with us. What a great turn of events. We all prayed together before we got on the elevator. I was letting the Holy Spirit guide my steps. I got off on the third floor with my interpreter, and two others got off too. The two of us turned to the left and walked to the end of the long hallway. We came to a larger room at the end of the hall with six beds in a row set against the back wall. I stopped at the door and looked in, and a woman was up on her bed crouched down. She was kind of growling or hissing. I walked over to her, and looking into her darkened eyes, I could see a demon. She had cuts on her arms from scratching herself.

I said everything through my interpreter.

I closed my eyes and laid my hand on her forehead and began to pray out loud.

As I was praying, I could feel a warm glow coming over us. I asked her what was wrong; she took my hand and placed it on her stomach where she had a large tumor. I could feel my hand sinking in. I closed my eyes and continued to pray.

I opened my eyes and looked with amazement at the transformation. It was like someone had poured syrup over this young woman. Her skin color was changing. She was glowing, and her eyes changed from black, dilated pupils to blue eyes. After about thirty seconds, I jumped back in amazement. I could not believe my eyes.

My interpreter said quaintly, "Mr. Don, I, from now on, go where you go."

The tumor that had been the size of a cinnamon roll was gone. She started jumping up and down on her bed and then in the hallway.

She yelled "Jesús! Jesús!" in Spanish.

She came back over to her bed, grabbed our Bible, and yelled out in Spanish, "I am to spread God's word everywhere I go!"

This is what I have experienced nearly everyone is saying after being transformed.

At that time, the other two people who got off on our floor came in and told us we had to leave because my interpreter and I were males, and this wing of the hospital was for women only. I had not noticed what was going on around me. This was where I was led to go.

In the main lobby, the rest of the group including the kids were still doing live skits. They had an amazing impact on the people who watched. Many people were saved.

Stepping out in faith and stepping out of your comfort zone lead to miraculous results. It does not matter who you are, what you have done, or what you have been ashamed of doing. God honors the faith you have now as a believer. He has a purpose for us all.

We were the first Americans who were ever given permission to go into this hospital. That was just the start of God opening doors for us everywhere we went. What a blessing. Again, God uses "people to reach people." He needs you to reach the people I will never see or be able to reach.

The hospital's director was very pleased with the response from the staff and the patients the day we were there. The crowds of people who gathered outside the hospital stayed for a long time, and they requested we keep speaking and interacting with the kids.

Hundreds of people were saved that day.

People need encouragement and uplifting spirits in their everyday lives. A great way to impact people is simply to smile and rejoice around them and show them love, God's love for one another. The spiritual part of traveling anywhere and impacting lives is you pray that after you leave, a local church will follow up with the people you have been impacting. The church needs to be Holy Spirit–filled to carry on the everyday and weekly discipleship of the people. New believers are hungry and excited to hear and learn more of God's word each day.

Think about it sometime: How many people do you see in a day or a week? The number might amaze you. You could change a lot of people's lives very easily. Because of your investment in their lives, they will not spend eternity in hell. Why do you think Satan and all his minions do everything they can to tell you, "You can't do this," "No way," and "Not"? Your friends, family, spouse, and kids, each of them is going somewhere, and who knows? Without your help, it probably will not be heaven. Just a thought.

Meanwhile, back at the ranch, we were the first Americans, again, to be given permission as a group to enter a prison in Costa Rica. You would not commit a crime again after being in this prison. First, the cells were disgusting. They had steel bunk beds around all the walls, and if everyone got onto the floor at the same time, they would not fit because it was that crowded.

All inmates got two meals a day, and none of the food was served with condiments. They received no toilet paper, no toothbrushes, no soap, no anything. If someone did not bring them for you from the outside, you didn't get them.

Chances were you would not get them anyway. We were told the guards kept everything of any value.

A small trough ran through the center of each cell in the cement floor. A small amount of water ran through it. You used that for everything, and I mean everything. It was bad, very bad. We got to meet with about fifteen inmates. They wore shackles. The warden arranged for the inmates and many guards to meet with us in a large, enclosed cement room. Armed guards were positioned everywhere.

No women were permitted in the prison.

That was a good thing because that would not have been a smart decision. Some of the guys with us brought a CD radio boom box and started break-dancing. These guys were good and had all the spins and moves. Then a couple inmates asked to be unchained to join in. The guards decided it was okay. That started a revival in that room. Everyone was clapping, and after about half an hour, we had a time of prayer and a time for sharing testimonies.

You could feel the power of the Holy Spirit fill the room. Many of the inmates accepted Jesus as their Lord and Savior. Believe it or not, several guards were saved too. Thank you, Jesus.

I had the opportunity to talk to several men. One was a young man who said he was from Panama.

He said, "I was arrested for drugs."

He told me he had been there for nearly a year, and they still had not even heard his case yet. This was not the place you would ever dream of being. That would be a nightmare from hell. Even that might be an understatement.

After being saved, another young man asked how he could find a church and get started to learn about the ministry after he got out of prison.

I told him, "Start your ministry now here in prison."

We gave out Bibles to the inmates and guards who wanted them. You have a captive audience in the prison, and you learn a lot about yourself in the process of ministering there. The Holy Spirit and God's word will give you guidance when you step out and minister in a place like that.

We had to wrap it up, turn off the music, and head back to the church. The prisoners were allotted only so much time out of their cells that day. God certainly moved the warden's heart and many others that day as well. We must have made a major impact on the guards and prisoners because two days later, the church received confirmation; they were given permission to come back again and share the Gospel with the prisoners and the guards. Amen.

Talk about stepping out in faith and breaking down major spiritual strongholds.

We had found when we got back home that the local church was setting up a schedule for the prison to accept regular visits from them.

The love of God is the key to every aspect of our lives. For any transformation to occur, it all starts with love first. I know, guys, this stops a lot of you right there in your tracks. No way. Not me. Have you ever heard the statement "real men love Jesus"? It is true. If you want healing, if you want prosperity, if you want anything biblical, it starts with Jesus's love and loving Jesus.

As the story goes, working every day, the wear and tear you feel from whatever can take its toll on all of us some time or another. To recharge yourself, the word of God—the Bible—your prayers, and the Holy Spirit, all give you the strength and guidance you need. Even on a mission trip, we were feeling the wear and tear, and the heat wore us down some days.

We had collected a love offering for the church where we stayed during our two weeks in Costa Rica. The women in the church worked very hard every day to prepare meals and do their work around the church. It came to our attention that the main stove in the kitchen at the church was beyond repair.

One of the women in our group said she had just been blessed before we left on the mission trip with a large sum of money from a relative. She decided to buy a stove for the church with her donation. Wow! Talk about awesome. A new gas stove there was very expensive. What a blessing it was for the church.

The church had been forced by the government to move from the building where they had originated to the building where they were in now. The lead pastor told us they had just moved about a month or so before we got there. The building they had found and were currently using had been a clothing store. It was a cement block building with only two windows on the front.

The church had set up classrooms on the first and second floor, with some chairs in each room. The rooms had no interior walls and no windows for the classrooms. It was not the best, but it was all they had. This was one of our projects as a team from the start: to build walls and to put in windows. We all got started building wood frames for each wall, standing them up and then drywalling each side. The materials were a lot different than we have in the United States.

Early the next morning, I was to head up the crew to put windows in the outside cement walls of each room on the second floor. We started hammering and chiseling all day long to create the openings for each window. Two guys who worked for the church maintenance crew were told to work with us to learn how to install new windows in the building. We were in for a big surprise that day.

I had my interpreter with me every day—yes, the same one.

He said, "We can walk to the store where we can buy all the materials we will need for the windows and to purchase the windows."

We had walked for several blocks when we came to a small storefront on a side street. We walked in, and I could not believe my eyes. It was as if we were back in the 1920s or 1930s here in the America.

There were bins everywhere with old-fashioned bolts, nuts, cut nails, and other supplies that were like they were from an old movie set in the early nineteen hundred.

I asked for shims and wood for trim around the windows. I had made a drawing and a material list for what we needed to get us through the project. The person working the only counter in the store said, "I will get your materials."

He was gone for a while, and when he returned, he had two rough lumber boards that were extremely crooked.

We tried to explain for about ten minutes that this was not what we needed. Well, this was all what we were going to get in the area of wood.

I started the process of explaining the length and width of the glass panes—for the windows we needed. Either double hung or single windows would be fine for a block building.

The individual said, "No problem," and walked away to the storage section of the store again!

For some reason, he would always take more than ten or fifteen minutes to return.

I never would have imagined he would return with a sheet of glass. That's right, a sheet of glass that was the same type of glass you would find in the early nineteen hundred in America.

This was what we ended up with to put windows in the school: several rough lumber boards—one by six by about eight feet long—and four panes of glass that were about two feet by three feet. We had to have an individual who was a glass cutter in the area cut the glass into the sizes we could use.

We talked for quite some time with the individual at the store, and we were told that was all they had in the way of windows. We walked back several times to pick up a chisel and drill bits to cut the remaining cement blocks.

I spent two days showing these guys how to cut the lumber to make window frames and to slot the wood for the glass. We made the window frames and framed in the openings. We had the glass for the windows cut by the local glass cutter so they would fit each of the windows we made.

We put latches on each window and made prop boards to hold the windows open.

The lead pastor and the teachers of the church were amazed at the progress we made and how the sunlight shining in each room brightened them up. The kids would sure enjoy having the rooms so much brighter.

We finished the drywall in each of the classrooms and painted each one to the color the church leaders had agreed to paint them.

The church had a large grassy backyard area that we used each day for outreach activities. We would set up games and activities for the families and children in the area. They were all welcomed to join in for fellowship, Bible times, and worship. We supplied food, Bibles, and treats for the kids. The church was making a great impact in the community. Amen.

A storm/hurricane had gone through Costa Rica about six months prior to us getting there. In a remote village about thirty miles from the church, the families waited for assistance from the government, but it had not arrived. Chances were they would never help them. The small villages were devastated. Their buildings were piles of rubble, with debris everywhere.

The people were living in cardboard shacks. For food, they walked all day through the surrounding areas looking for scraps in dumpsters or whatever they could find. We spent some time witnessing, talking, and listening to the people in the area. Many people got saved that day. We left everything we could and gave them food, Bibles, blankets, clothes, and the continued support of prayers.

We take so much for granted sometimes. We forget just how fortunate we are. The freedom that we have and the prosperity we enjoy are priceless. A lot of people have died to make our country free, and we are blessed to be a Christian nation in America.

The mission trip was coming to an end.

That thing on the wall sure does go fast at times. I think it jumps forward at times when we are not looking.

As years go by in our family, I think months and years just fly by.

I could go on and quote all kinds of Bible verses, and they are all important in explaining how this lines up with God's word. Do not get me wrong, it is the most powerful thing on the planet. You have to search for yourself or it will not matter where it really counts—your heart. Your mind is already full of enough stuff you hear and watch every day and night. Our culture here in America is the place to be desensitized. Stop reading for a moment and think how much influence you receive every day from the radio, computers, cell phones, television, and on and on. Oh, wait, "I'm too busy. Do not bother me."

Of the twenty-four hours each day, we spend about sixteen hours awake. Multiply that by seven, then by 365.25 (leap year). Wow! That is a lot of time for your mind to grasp things. There's hope though, and it is very simple. Make a couple changes, get into a space suit, board a spaceship, and take off. Walhalla!

Your troubles are over. Not. Seriously though, take a little time each night or morning and read your Bible. Start in Matthew and read the New Testament. It is important to read out loud to yourself or your spouse, if you're married, or to your friends. This is so powerful and simple. It takes very little time.

I guarantee your spirit will change. Find a good Holy Spirit–filled church. Meeting with other believers brings new life to your bones. Ask Ezekiel some time. You might even decide to sing out loud when no one is looking. You're one bright day in the middle of the night will change your life forever.

12

He Will Get Your Attention

It was a fall day, and our family was going in opposite directions for church services on a given Sundays. My wife and oldest son were volunteering at a new start-up church close to home. I was taking the rest of our clan and commuting to several other churches to help with their needs.

At the time, we were attending one of the large denominational churches in our area. During the service, the pastor, a friend of mine, asked the congregation for prayers for a pastor who was fighting for his life from a disease that had set into his body. The Holy Spirit gave me an inclination to call on the pastor and ask if he had time to meet.

I prayed and asked for guidance and wisdom to reach out to help a brother with his needs.

Well, when God is involved and I mean the God with a big G—not the god of this world, Satan, with a little g—things happen.

I called the pastor, and we talked for quite some time. We set a time to meet for lunch the next week. He sure had a lot going on in his life.

The pastor was a family man. He had two boys who were the same age as two of our boys. He was on crutches because of extensive surgeries on his legs. The church he was pastoring was going through a new start-up in an abandoned chain store in the neighborhood where he had grown up as a kid. This was a high-crime area and was a predominately African American community. I was amazed at how God works. This was only blocks away from the high-rise I supervised the building project for many years ago when I first moved to the area.

We talked for hours, and it seemed as though we had been best friends for a lifetime. Sometimes when we look back, we see that our God's plans for us are amazing. This being the same neighborhood I spent a lot of time in many years ago made it easy to know my way around.

Some of the local stores and small food shops where we had ordered food many years ago were still there. Over the course of several months, we ate breakfast and lunch together when we could, setting an agenda for individuals who needed help and prayers.

We had several meetings with other leaders in the church about getting the building ready for services on Sundays. We held Bible study classes on Wednesday evenings and outreaches and street ministries on Friday evenings.

My family looked forward to this each week. We became very close to many homeless people, and we got to know a lot of people on the streets. It is amazing to see how God takes away all barriers when we let go and spread His love openly and willingly.

Barriers existed between the board members and other church leaders. This carried over to the families in the church, which was not good. The board was mostly made up of denominational leaders, some who were retired and full of religion. The pastor was on fire with the Holy Spirit; he wanted so badly to spread God's word to the people. Sounds like the church in Ephesus.

Once again, the church would be a very easy place to work, if not for all the people. Amazing.

Three pastors spoke on Sundays and helped in all areas while the lead pastor was unable to have enough strength to make it in each week due to his sickness and treatments.

One Sunday, as I was sitting with my wife in the second row during the service, Pastor Derick said during his sermon, "God is going to punish you for your sins, and that car accident that happened last week was God's punishment. Isn't that right, Pastor?" He asked as he pointed to me.

I was stunned and brokenhearted. I could feel the flesh side of me getting the better of me, so I had to calm down. All we had worked for to explain God's love and what the Bible said had crashed and burned in that one statement from Pastor Derick.

I waited to talk with Pastor Derick after the service, and I asked, "Where in the Bible did you get that?"

I was surely interested to see what he had to say. He showed me four different verses that spoke about God's wrath and punishment.

I was surprised how he as a pastor had come to this conclusion. I asked him to read before and after each verse to see the context leading up to and following to get some additional meaning to the verbiage used in each verse.

I also said I was going to make it very clear to the congregation I did not support such a negative claim to Jesus's love and kindness to us.

You can see how quickly we can get sidetracked and led astray even in church. I have been in well over fifty churches, and it amazes me to see the different personalities and doctrines in some churches. To make it very simple: The Bible must be the road map for all churches. End of discussion. The whole Bible, not just bits and pieces or only certain books.

As Bob Yandian often said at the pastor conferences we attended, "Jesus is the ultimate power." This is so very true. You must first know who and what you are dealing with here. Satan is the great deceiver. He comes to steal, kill, and destroy.

His first act as the fallen angel was to overcome Eve and then Adam. His plans were to deceive them. The key word here is to deceive Eve, then Adam. As the demon said, "I know your steps before you take them." We are known to be creatures of habit.

As you read in one of the last chapters where everyone is spending way too much of their time and millions of dollars being deceived again by Satan's demons in trying desperately to get all the religious material, plaques, etc. out of post offices, schools, etc. when our churches should be our focus regarding nativity scenes, Ten Commandments displays, etc. Our churches are being neglected everywhere all the time. The jerk deceiver is at work again.

Most of us know we live in a sin-based world, and we must live with this every day. Jesus is the answer to our prayers. We must rely on Jesus using our faith. To take this one step further, the Bible tells us clearly throughout that our sins are what puts us in our own situations.

As spring came, I was injured in an accident. I had several discs dislocated in my neck. It had laid me up for a while. The pain I went through was unbearable. I cannot even put it into words.

Later in the spring, a pastors' conference in the Midwest at Branson we have attended in the spring every year gave us the opportunity to drive to the conference and visit Grandma on our way back. She lived only around two hours from the conference.

We all looked forward to the time, which was well spent at both places. It was like getting our batteries recharged. I had been in an accident on a machine I was running.

I messed up some discs in my neck, and it felt as if someone was stabbing me with a knife. This was not caused by God. After the accident happened, several months had gone by.

The person I was working for excavating on their property was a member of an atheistic cult with a large following. Imagine that. Some things are not just coincidences. I was not aware of this until sometime later.

One thing was I broke down physically. When the Holy Spirit is involved, sometimes you find yourself crying with nearly endless tears. It seems like a cleansing of emotions and pain. Sometimes you must let go and truly let God work in your life; guys, it is hard.

He had my undivided attention again. All He was asking was for a little respect and a little time and, with it, focus only on Him. That is called being a good Father.

God had my attention after all this pain and misdirection from the toad called Satan. I have learned over the years that if you want answers from the Big Guy, God, all you must do is ask, prayers. The hard part is being patient for the answers.

They do not always come in the form of words; sometimes they come through people or sometimes through dreams.

I prayed to God, "Why is it that John Lake, Smith Wigglesworth, or Kenneth Hagin healed people and raised them from the dead? What am I not seeing in people that these guys could see and I could not?"

Every time I have prayed for answers, I have always received answers I would never have guessed. The answers must line up with God's word, the Bible, or you can pitch them because they are not from Him.

Several nights in a row, I had dreams that were so vivid and real. In the first dream, I could see people who were sick and people who were struggling with sin in their lives. The next night, I saw people's lives being cut short, being burdened down with sadness and sicknesses again. The third night was nearly too much to handle. First, I cannot stand snakes. I am not afraid of them. I just cannot stand them. Maybe it's because I was bitten by a rattle snake once when I was blueberry picking in the mountains many years back.

I can remember my dream all too well. There was a snake slithering in a tree. It was a large python boa constrictor type with bright-red eyes. I could see people walking around with snakes circling them everywhere they went.

I could see some of them getting weaker and tired as the snake curled tighter around their body, starting to choke them. Then there was a large snake above me in the tree; it was slithering and circling me. It wrapped itself around me, and how gross, it was touching me, and as it squeezed, it started getting tighter. I could feel the skin of the snake on me as it got tighter and tighter.

I woke up in a sweat, and I was creeped out to the max. I sat on the edge of the bed for a little while to try to shake off the creepy feeling. Then I went into the bathroom to wash my face and try again to get rid of that creepy snake feeling. It was three-fifteen in the morning.

Three or four weeks went by, and I was in the southern part of the city, at a local supply yard. I got out of my truck and was going into the office when an elderly Black man was coming out and bumped into me. As he bumped into me, I felt something. He turned, came back, and talked to me, and we talked for a while. I felt this person needed help with something—perhaps he needed me to witness to him—and we spoke. I prayed over him and gave him a hug. When I gave him a hug, I felt that warm, creepy feeling; it was like a snake was crawling around me. I jumped back.

He looked at me and asked, "What's wrong?"

I was stunned for a minute. I didn't know what to say. We shook hands and parted ways.

Several months went by, and I got a phone call one day. He told me that the guy that I spoke to, the pastor at the supply yard, had said he was dying of cancer and that after I prayed over him in Jesus's name, he had been completely healed of cancer.

He said, "Thank you so very much."

I said, "It wasn't me. It was Jesus."

He thanked me again and said that his life had been saved. He said he was going to spread God's Word every place he went.

About a month went by, and I laid down and dreamed again. I was walking and being told, "Now you can see what your world is made up of. The sin you have, as it gets greater, so does the hold on you from the serpent get tighter. Whether it be in the form of sickness or death, the hold on you from the serpent is from your sins."

God said, "You have the power and authority. Use it. Do not be deceived. People ask me to remove the sickness or disease. They are the ones who sinned. They have the same power as believers and authority even greater because. I am here with the Father [Jesus]."

Again, do not be deceived.

Probably the greatest deceiver in our lifetime is Benedict (Arnold) Pence deceiving our nation and his peers.

Ending a book on this topic is challenging because there are so many aspects of God's work that people should be aware of. One important topic is understanding the fundamentals which is very important because it allows us to see how certain companies, especially one in particular, introduce harmful bioengineered food products added into our food. This practice has contributed to making the United States one of the sickest countries with the highest rates of cancer and other diseases, a trend that began in the '80s and '90s. This was evident from the testing in South America and two other labs. The difficulty in tracing these chemicals arises when they are introduced into one food product and then another, each with a different chemical composition. The combination of these chemicals will lead to health issues. Moreover, they profit from the drugs advertised in commercials, which are purported to restore health, despite all the side effects.

Equally important is to know who is educating your children in schools. You would be surprised at what's coming out of the counselors' and teachers' mouths—I've seen it firsthand in schools—and then the leading of kids to homosexuality and all the gay and perverted things going on, swaying our kids. What can be done? Pray, find a supportive church, and remember that faith without works is dead. It's crucial to participate in school boards and engage with your community, townships, and state. Individuals in positions of authority—including school board members, senators, and others in different positions and with different principles—are pushing the agendas. The best way to fight back is to get involved. Have a blessed day.

Conclusion

Today we have a 4G network and a 5G network. The clarity and the speed are amazing to see and hear. The network you have been reading and learning is the network that God created for you, a person who knows and understands the difference in the one network and the other. That is right, you, your spirit and soul, either belong to the network of this world or of the world of believers in Jesus; the Holy Jesus's network will prolong your life on into eternity. This is the spiritual side of your life. This is a totally different wavelength than the 5G or 4G network you are used to hearing about.

The physical side of your life: You take vitamins, exercise, get Botox treatments, plastic surgery, all to look good and try to prolong your life. Well, the best way to prolong your life and live forever is to accept Jesus as your Lord and Savior and live for eternity in heaven. No cost, no expense at all. You have nothing to lose and everything to gain. Just a thought though: I would believe it will extend your life here. You decide.

People must learn to let God work in their hearts.

To do that, you must be a member of the family of believers. The only way to the Father is through the Son.

God always has plans for us, and sometimes we have no clue. That might be for the best sometimes, but His plans include being adventurous, finding a church, and attending regularly. Being water baptized and speaking in tongues are the greatest things you can do for yourself since apple pie and ice cream. Do not check out just yet. There is still one thing missing.

Have you ever heard about the traveling salesman who drove into a small town and saw a little boy standing on the corner? He said, "Son, do you know where there's a good restaurant?"

The boy replied, "No, sir."

"Do you know where the local garage is?"

The little boy replied, "No, sir."

"Do you know where the motel is?"

The boy replied, "No, sir."

Finally, out of frustration, the salesman asked, "Do you know anything, boy?"

The boy replied, "I'm not the one that is lost, mister."

In 1 Corinthians 13:12, the Bible says, "Now, I know in part, but then I shall know…" You are going to have a lot of questions thrown at you in these latter days, and you may not have all the answers, but one thing you can tell them—you're not lost.

Accept Jesus now and know where you are going. Start your life over with a new beginning. You are born again when you accept Jesus as your Lord and Savior. Do not look back at what you did; move forward. How great is that for all of us?

After reading all this, I hope you can see how "having God in your life," makes a world of difference.

One bright day in the middle of the night.

There are steps you can take to help you in your life. Whether you are young or old, White or Black, rich or poor, it does not matter. Your inner self, your spirit, is what matters. A lot of good books and information are out there. Remember though, know the Bible first.

Consider this: We read in the book of Acts that Paul was saved. If Paul could be saved from all he did to have Christians killed and persecuted, then you are entitled to the same forgiveness.

If you are reading books or getting any "helpful" advice and it does not line up with the Bible, then pitch the book. Do not read it unless you know you are reading fiction. Then it's okay.

When you are alone at work or driving or you might be in front of a mirror or getting ready to sack out, speak out loud to God. Talk to Him. Do this daily. He is your Father who loves you. Pray in Jesus's name. Your words are powerful.

Just a thought: God spoke the world into existence. Key word here: spoke. Your spiritual power as a believer is the same as Jesus's. Use your words.

Guys, do not check out at this point. You are not weak or weird by engaging in the love. Remember, He is your Father. He is a Father who forgives you of whatever might be in your closet. I guarantee He will hear you and forgive you when you "truly repent" in Jesus's name.

The one bright day in the middle of the night, the start of the first day was evening. That was the custom in biblical times. When you decide to make Jesus your Lord and Savior, that is your one bright day in the middle of your night.

Darkness will be gone, and Jesus in you makes "you the light" to bring a bright day so you can bring light to someone else in the middle of their night.

"Always Remember You Are Blessed and Highly Favored."
Say that each day, "I Am Blessed and Highly Favored."
God Bless. May the Faith Be With You.

About the Author

The life and times of this book are true to myself. I can look back and see it is not a coincidence that I always seemed to be where there was a person or situation that needed to be changed for the better or revealed. My hope is that people can see that an everyday person can make a difference by having faith with works. John is looking forward to more speaking engagements at churches or events on the book/healing.